DOWN TO EARTH

Faith Addis

Down to Earth

ANDRE DEUTSCH

First published in Great Britain April 1987
by André Deutsch Ltd
105-106 Great Russell Street, London WC1B 3LJ
Second impression September 1987

Typeset by Falcon Graphic Art Ltd
Wallington, Surrey
Printed in Great Britain by
Ebenezer Baylis & Son Ltd, Worcester

British Library Cataloguing in Publication Data

Addis, Faith
  Down to earth
  1. Horticulture——England
  I. Title
  635'.092'4   SB319.3.G7

ISBN 0–233–98046–6

To Grace

Chapter One

Dear Brian,

The course is hard work but good fun. There are twenty of us – ten advanced and ten beginners including me and two teachers. My group's teacher is quite strict which I suppose is a good thing when you're responsible for seeing that other people's pets don't get cut to ribbons. She's a Cockney girl in her mid-twenties and she's got an Alf Garnett way of referring to 'your' this and that. She shouted 'mind yer testicles' to one of the advanced pupils who was getting careless round the rear end of an Old English sheepdog and I had a job to keep a straight face. I've been on paws all day which is fiddly but not dangerous like testicles . . .

Dear Faith,

What do you mean am I eating properly? Surely any fool can defrost a cooked casserole. The liver was on the dry side though and I would have liked some bacon with it but I fried a couple of rashers and it was OK.

Glad to hear you are enjoying yourself. Do you really have to spend £121 plus VAT on equipment? How about getting it second-hand?

P.S. Honey was sick. I didn't know you gave the dogs onions.

NO, BRIAN AND I weren't writing to each other because we had split up (although if he and the dogs continued to eat each other's freezer meals it wouldn't be long) but because he was holding the fort while I was away on a course. The Canine Beauticians' Course Part One to be precise.

There are many dog-grooming schools throughout Britain and I had chosen one in London which was reputed to be one of the best. It was a residential course but the proprietors didn't mind if some of us lived out and I was lucky enough to be able to stay with Sue and Keith, some friends of ours who lived near the school.

I hurried along the street thinking how dirty London pavements had become since I was last there seven years ago. Kentucky Chicken cartons, cigarette packets and discarded tissues blew about untidily in the cold December wind. Even though I was enjoying the dog course I longed to be back in Devon's clear air . . .

'Hi, Faith.' A girl called Colette, a fellow Part-One pupil, hopped off a double-decker. 'You look a bit serious – Giro not come?' Colette was under the heel of the SS (Social Security) and suffered fortnightly cycles of anxiety that they would forget to send her money.

'Hullo, Colette.' We walked along together and I told her about Brian eating the dogs' liver and she told me about an injured kestrel she knew that had eaten its own gangrenous foot with no ill effects.

It was cold in the beauty parlour and would remain so until the first dogs emerged from their baths. Then the big commercial driers would be switched on and the place would become like a sauna. After we had all changed into our overalls Alison, our teacher, called the register. As we answered she called out the names of the dogs we had each been allocated for the morning session. Every dog had two names, its own Christian name and its owner's surname. This was an important part of the procedure as it was quite common to find two or three dogs with the same name. Prince, for example, was a popular name but if Prince Walters, a Lakeland terrier, was mistaken for Prince Sinclair, a Welsh terrier, there could be some awfully cross owners at the end of the day. (Lakelands have their stomachs clipped but the Welsh remain fully clothed below shoulder level.)

The first two days of the course had been devoted to paws – care of and shaping of – and to bathing and blow-drying techniques. Now on our third day we were to do whole dogs from soup to nuts.

I was paired with Max Green for the morning lesson and

Max Green had seen it all before. He was a six-year-old black miniature poodle and had been coming to the salon for years. Alison always tried to give the beginners 'easy' dogs to start with and she made sure I had got Max firmly secured on a bench before she moved along the line to the next pupil.

'Good morning, Max,' I said respectfully. He was a classy little dog and a formal approach seemed appropriate. 'Would you mind if I, um, move you forward a bit?' Max summed me up in a flash and sat down. Tentatively I put my hand under his rump and stood him up again.

'Not like that.' Alison was at my side again.

'Stand up, Max,' she commanded. Max sprang to attention.

'Take his chain up three links,' she said and moved off again.

The dogs were held in place by thick chains suspended from hooks in the ceiling. One chain went round the dog's stomach and was clipped back on itself and the other one was looped round the neck and secured in the same way. The reason for thick rather than thin chains was to prevent chafing or cutting if the dog got too lively.

I took up the slack in Max's hind chain so that now he had no choice but to stand. He gave me a rueful look as if to say 'Well, it was worth a try' then together we studied his card:

Poodle. Max Green. Style: Lamb Clip.
1 Clip 4 paws
2 Clip face
3 Clip back and sides
4 Brush all over
5 Bath and empty anal glands
6 Blow-dry and brush out
7 Comb legs and scissor to shape
8 Comb tail and topknot and scissor to shape
9 Cut nails
10 Comb out and leave on clean surface. Do not handle coat

I had just four hours to complete these ten stages, about twice as long as it would take an experienced operator. With two days' paw practice behind me, it didn't take long to remove all the fur on Max's feet. Some dogs are ticklish between the toes but Max was a wonderfully co-operative partner and stood patiently on three legs as I dealt with each paw in turn.

Alison supervised his face clipping and tidied up the tufts of fur I had missed. Then she asked one of the advanced pupils to guide me through the body clip. Poor Max looked a real mess when I had finished, like a lawn covered in molehills.

'I seem to have missed quite a lot,' I apologised. 'It's harder than it looks, isn't it?'

'It's not too bad for a first go,' said the girl kindly. She took the clippers from me and skilfully whizzed over Max's ribs until the whole area was uniform. Watching her, I could see what I had been doing wrong; I hadn't been pulling the skin taut enough. When men shave they don't just scrape round all the lumps and bumps in their faces, they pull awkward bits this way and that until they have a flat area to work on. Dog clipping requires a similar technique.

Alison clapped her hands for silence. 'Right, girls. Would all the beginners take a coffee break, please. What have you got to remember before you leave the room?'

'Safety check,' we all chorused. It sounded like a revivalist meeting – the Sisterhood of Canine Beauticians.

'Ten minutes then.' The salon machinery hummed back into action.

'I'm going for some coffee, Max,' I said. He wagged his tail. 'I'll see if I can get you some chocolate.' I unhooked his stomach chain and loosened his neck chain five links. Gratefully he lay down and put his head on his paws. He had been standing for over an hour and a half and deserved a break. Safety check next, switch off the electric plug, make sure chain is slack enough for dog to lie down but not long enough for it to leap off the bench (dogs had been known to break their necks in some salons, according to Alison), and remove all sharp tools to the shelves below the bench.

The students were provided with a sitting room where you could have a wash, a cup of coffee and a natter. We collected our drinks and swapped notes. Colette had been bitten by Twinkle Miller and another girl called Evelyn had used the wrong blade on Cherie Delavigne, turning what should have been a lamb clip (the same style that I was working on) into a shape called Dutch. This wouldn't have mattered all that much as the customers got their treatments at half price in return for letting us beginners loose on them, but in Cherie's case she was accompanied by her (dog) mother, Chantelle. Their owner liked to have them looking the same so now Chantelle would have to have a Dutch clip too.

These two minor mishaps apart, the first attempts at whole dogs were going well. We weren't even put off by dark hints like 'You wait until you start on terriers' from a gloom-monger in the advanced class.

Max was asleep when I returned to my bench so I prodded him awake and gave him a piece of Kit Kat. His pleasure was short-lived however as the next item on the agenda was his bath and dogs, in common with small boys, are not exactly wild about washing.

The baths were ordinary human ones mounted on blocks so that we could work without bending and with rubber mats in the bottom to stop the dogs skidding about. Max flattened himself on one of the mats and remained a picture of misery until I had shampooed and rinsed him twice and applied conditioner. I wrapped him in a towel and lifted him out.

'You've forgotten yer anal glands,' said the hawk-eyed Alison. I hadn't but I hoped nobody had noticed. I thought, and I still think, that emptying other people's dogs' anal glands is not a job for the novice. But all Alison's customers had to have it done willy-nilly. Dear patient Max found himself back in the bath, glands emptied on to a piece of cotton wool and another rinse beneath the tail.

'You've done this before, haven't you?' said Alison, making it sound like some great treat I was keeping all to myself.

'I've got three dogs of my own,' I said. 'An old mongrel, a Cavalier and a collie. I see to the old dog's glands about once a year but the younger ones don't have any problems.'

'Once a year isn't enough,' said Alison briskly. I thought of an apt one-word retort to this but since I didn't want to be thrown out on my ear on the third day I shut up and carried Max back to a drying bench.

Each drying area was supplied with two large floor-mounted hair driers which swivelled independently so that you could direct two cross-jets of warm air at the exact spot you were working on. With poodles we were taught to blow-dry one leg at a time, combing the fur upwards all the time to create a fluffy candy-floss effect. Then we had to do the topknot, tail and body. We learned that some salons (presumably the same ones that let the dogs jump off benches and strangle themselves) used cage driers. Here the dog is shut in a wire cage and subjected to near-suffocation as hot air envelops it. We all promised never to use cage driers.

By noon Max's fur was dry. This left one hour before the lunch break to scissor him into the required 'lamb' shape and to cut his nails. Years of hedge-cutting practice made the soft poodle fur a piece of cake and soon I had him sculpted like the illustration on the wall chart in front of me. I was about to cut his nails when one of the advanced students stopped me. 'You're not allowed to do black dogs' nails in your first week,' she said. 'I'll find you a white one to practise on.'

'What's she talking about?' I whispered to the girl in the next cubicle. But she was having problems of her own in the shape of Buttons Parker, an overweight standard poodle who kept dribbling, so she wasn't able to enlighten me.

The advanced girl came back with a white Peke and sat it on my bench. 'White dog, white nails,' she explained, 'and white nails are transparent. There's no danger of you cutting too much off because you can see the blood vessel inside.' Then she showed me how to trim a town dog's nails. 'Just the tip off,' she said. 'They're on pavements such a lot of the time the nails hardly ever get overgrown.'

I was very glad of the demonstration because, left to my own devices, I could easily have cut too much off. Country-reared dogs, exercised mainly on grass, have to have a good quarter of an inch off their nails every six weeks or so and it had not occurred to me that town dogs would be any different.

I watched the girl cut the Peke's front nails, then I did the back ones. She had a look at Max's and decided they only needed a quick rasp with a sandpaper file. Max, sensing that his time was nearly up, continued to be wholly co-operative so I gave him the rest of the Kit Kat. Then I lifted him down and put him in the 'clean' cage, a large playpen affair where all the finished dogs were put to wait for their owners to collect them. Well-behaved dogs like Max were allowed loose in the pen but tetchy ones had to be tied up to rings in the wall. One by one the pen filled up with sweet-smelling dogs.

Soon the owners, most of whom had also spent the morning at the hairdresser's, filed in. The dogs went wild with excitement and the room rang with ecstatic yelps as pets and owners were reunited.

In the afternoon we all did another dog apiece. By five thirty we were thankful to hand them over to the advanced girls to finish. Two four-hour sessions standing at a bench had made our legs ache and we were dying to sit down with a cup of tea. After we had removed our overalls and tidied up, the residential girls (we were all 'girls' even though our ages ranged from eighteen to sixty-three) disappeared into their sitting room while the rest of us headed for the bus stop. Someone said, 'Anyone seen the list for tomorrow? There's a Doberman called Satan Bingley. Can't say I fancy tackling *his* toenails.' We all laughed and a tiny birdlike girl called Peggy who was about four feet ten gave a nervous giggle and said it would be just her luck to get him.

The evening was raw and foggy and it was a relief to get back to Sue and Keith's warm house. Sue, who bred pedigree cats, was mixing kitten feeds in the kitchen, the two children Lauren and Jordan were getting undressed in the bathroom and Keith was still out at work.

'Did you have a good day?' asked Sue.

'Very. Quite tiring though. How about you?'

'Not bad. I'm thinking of hiring myself out to the police as a crowd-control expert.' She indicated the thronging cats and kittens at her feet, fourteen altogether, the smallest kittens squeaking with impatience as they tried to scale her jeans.

'Can I help?' I detached two minuscule bodies from her leg and held them against my face. Their fur was as soft as cashmere and had that lovely brand-new smell peculiar to all young animals. Most of Sue's cats were Colourpoint – a long-haired, square-faced breed ranging in colour from white (like the cat in the carpet adverts) to Smoke, a subtle mixture of browns and slate greys. The two I was holding were four-week-old Smokes, each worth a small fortune even though they weren't much bigger than caterpillars. Sue said she didn't need a hand with the feeds but would be glad if I could run a bath for the children. I made myself a cup of tea and took it upstairs to the bathroom.

'Oh good, it's Fafe,' said Lauren. She was three, an age group with which I feel completely at home. 'Can we have Evil Edna tonight, Fafe?'

'What's Evil Edna?' I said, capturing baby Jordan who was trying to crawl towards the open door.

'She's a witch. She does bad fings.'

'Finish getting undressed and I'll think about it,' I said. I had done two stints of Mr Men and Postman Pat and had rather been looking forward to something demanding like *The House at Pooh Corner*.

Lauren climbed into the bath and pulled all the water toys in after her. Jordan let me peel his nappy off without protest and I plonked him in too.

'He's supposed to go at the other end,' Lauren said. 'Because of hitting his head on the taps.' The children slithered past each other with much giggling and started to play.

'I did bulgy at school today,' said Lauren proudly. 'Did you do bulgy at your school, Fafe? Did Brian do bulgy? Did Marcus and Sara— '

'Yes,' I said quickly, hoping bulgy wasn't one of those subjects which had only just been invented. (Three half-days a week Lauren went to a kindergarten where, if Lauren was anything to go by, the educational standards were very high indeed.) 'What else did you do today?'

'I did L for Lauren and E for Edward. Edward sat next to me but I don't want to marry him.'

'No?'

'No, he sucks his thumb and he's four.'

I wasn't sure whether she meant it was Edward's great age or his thumb-sucking which made him poor husband material but I agreed that she was wise not to commit herself too soon.

8

When Sue came up later she found both children still unwashed and their minder engrossed in Evil Edna. What appealed to me, as a non-addict of television, was that Edna always had to turn herself into a TV set before her bad magic could work.

'We were getting bored with Postman Pat,' I said, feeling guilty as though I had been giving the children sweets in bed. 'Sue – what's bulgy?'

'Biology. This term it's a hyacinth bulb in a growing jar.'

'I'm behind the times. I did cress on a flannel at her age.'

'Me too. Or was it beans on blotting paper? I think Lauren's class is doing open-heart surgery next term.'

'We're doing frog spawn, silly,' Lauren said. 'It turns into, er, what does it turn into, Mummy?'

Sue described a tadpole, then immediately regretted it as Lauren insisted on being a tadpole before she got into bed. With both legs inside one leg of her pyjama bottoms she wriggled across the floor. Jordan didn't want to be a tadpole but he didn't want his nappy on either and Sue had to put one knee on his chest before she could parcel him up ready for his cot. Then Lauren had to be persuaded that tadpoles slept lying down like everyone else and what with one thing and another it was quite late before both children were battened down for the night.

Even then there were still more baths to come. After supper Sue had to bath two of her cats who were going to a show in a few days' time. I acted as under-nanny, handing the towels as required. Until then I hadn't known you have to bath show cats or that it's such an easy operation, a one-shampoo one-rinse job followed by a blow-dry on the draining board. Both cats were used to it and were perfectly docile the whole time. What really surprised me was that when they were done they didn't immediately look for something nasty to roll in (as dogs do) but moved off, calm and dignified like the Queen Mother. I don't think I have ever participated in so many baths in one day, seven altogether – two dogs, two children, two cats and then self at eleven o'clock. Shampoo manufacturers must all be millionaires.

Next day, back at the dog salon, it all started again. Still chuckling at the memory of Lauren's breakfast-time 'rehearsal' for her part in the end of term entertainment ('I'm a little teapot short and stout,' she declaimed earnestly, placing one hand on a non-existent hip and raising the other in what she imagined to be a graceful curve. 'Tip me up and pour me out.') I rolled up my sleeves and waited to see who was going to be my dog partner for the morning session.

Alison called the beginners' register and the dog register: Tango Brookman, Satan Bingley, Coco Fields, Daisy Morris, Smudge MacDonald, Milo Copeland, Rex Harrison, Ellie Jones, Holly O'Reilly and Samuel Samuelson. Samuel was a Yorkshire terrier and a most popular dog because his owner, a regular customer, always left a large piece of delicious homemade cheesecake for his elevenses which was bad for a small dog but wonderful shared out among ten novice beauticians. Some of the other owners left doggy choc drops which were better than nothing but not a patch on Mrs Samuelson's cooking. The worst owners as far as we were concerned were the ones who left Shapes or Bonios.

Satan Bingley, the Doberman that tiny Peggy had been afraid would be allocated to her, was handed over to an advanced pupil. We thought this was because he was too savage for a beginner but it turned out that Satan, despite his macho studded collar and thonged lead, was about as savage as a butterfly and unless he was handled with great tact and kindness would wet himself with fright. Like Samuel, Satan was a regular, coming in every fortnight for a bath. His owner, a gentle boy of sixteen who was going to be a world famous pop star as soon as he had finished his O levels, wasn't allowed to bath Satan at home because of the mess.

Rex Harrison on the other hand was a horror, an enormous Airedale who had been allowed to rule the roost at home and whose owner 'couldn't do a thing with him'. Hairballs as big as pincushions had formed in his chest and armpits and his rear end was matted with dried muck. We all stared at him apprehensively. He stared right back and growled.

'That's enough of *that*, Rex,' Alison said firmly and hit him on the nose with a rolled-up newspaper. 'You're going to be bathed and clipped and you're going to be a good boy. OK?'

'Who's going to do him, Alison?' we asked, retreating out of range of the now snapping teeth.

The answer, dismayingly, was that we all were. Not all at once, though I don't doubt Rex could have crunched his way through the lot of us, but in pairs – 'So that you all get some practice on a difficult dog.' It seemed the salon didn't often get a really bad case so we must make the most of this rare opportunity.

While Rex was being put on the 'rack', a rubber-based bench that could be jacked up and down to suit the operator's height, we all started on our own dogs. I had an affectionate Sealyham called Smudge MacDonald. He wagged his stump of a tail so much I had a job to hold his body steady for the clippers but eventually we came to an understanding. Then just as I was getting on nicely Alison called me out for my stint on Rex.

'Stand on his left side,' she commanded, 'and you, Ruby, here on his right.' Ruby, an elderly woman who had only come on the dog course to learn how to show-clip Bedlingtons, moved in nervously. 'The first two girls have tidied up his back end,' Alison went on, 'so I want you two to scissor out all the matts in his chest and neck. You can have half an hour.'

I shan't forget our half hour with Rex Harrison in a hurry. His eyes gleamed with menace as he sized us up and his breath was hot. He seemed undecided whether to have Ruby's jugular first or mine; his large and perfect teeth were like a gin trap in good working order. Cautiously, Ruby and I inched towards him holding our scissors out in front of us like exorcists . . .

'WOOF,' said Rex in a huge bass voice. Ruby screamed and fled to the rest room for her Valium.

'Oh really,' said Alison crossly, 'you mustn't let him get the upper hand.' Everyone howled with laughter at this appropriate choice of phrase and Rex, enjoying the limelight, barked again. Some of the other dogs joined in.

'Do you *mind*,' said the girl who was bathing Satan Bingley. 'You're making such a row Satan's trembling.'

Ruby came back and took up her position at Rex's head.

11

'You OK, Ruby?' Alison asked. Ruby nodded. 'Right,' said Alison. 'Let's start again. The thing is, you mustn't let a dog suspect you're afraid or it makes it worse. Rex can't actually bite you, you know – I've hooked his head up so tightly he hasn't got much range of movement so you're quite safe.'

Ruby and I checked that the overhead hooks and chains were indeed tight before we started on the hairballs. At first Rex struggled but Alison shook him by the scruff every time he snapped and after a while he calmed down. Then Alison had to leave us to carry on without her as Colette was calling for help. 'Oh God, she's been bitten again,' said Alison. 'What's wrong with the girl – two days running she's been bitten.'

It appeared that Daisy Morris, a small white poodle, had taken a leaf out of Rex Harrison's book and had attempted to have Colette's fingers for elevenses.

'You've got blood on your fur,' Alison accused Colette, and whisked Daisy Morris under the cold-water tap. 'I've told you time and again not to stain white fur – the owners don't like it. Now get a plaster for that finger quick, and wipe your bench.'

'I can hardly believe we're paying to do this,' Ruby observed as she clipped out the umpteenth matt on Rex's chest. She seemed to have lost her earlier nervousness.

'How long do those Valium things of yours take to work?' I asked curiously.

Ruby looked round to see if anyone was listening. 'Not long,' she whispered. 'I gave him two.'

The days sped by and soon we beginners were promoted to mongrels. Mongrels can be harder to clip than pure-breds because you have no textbook guidelines to show you what shape your dog should be when you've finished. Alison told us to aim for the breed that the dog most nearly resembles but she overlooked the fact that, artistically speaking, no two people will ever 'see' the same thing.

On the first mongrel day she stopped by Peggy's bench and exclaimed 'Blimey, Peggy – what the hell's that supposed to be?' Peggy's dog which had lumbered in looking like a Russian peasant was beginning to look like the female half of a Come Dancing partnership. Soft grey fur frothed around his legs to reveal the canine equivalent of slim ankles. 'His owner'll go mad,' Alison said. 'You've made him look like a poof.'

'Him?' said Peggy. 'I thought he was a her.'

'What do you mean you thought he was a her? Didn't you *feel*?' Alison groped under the dog's skirts and gave Peggy a rather generalised description of what she called a male's 'equipment'. Peggy said if Alison's husband kept his equipment half-way along his stomach he should see a doctor. 'And anyway, how was I to know he was a boy?' she said defensively. 'Cass is a girl's name.'

'Cass is short for Cassius, you nit,' said Alison. 'Didn't you do Shakespeare?'

Peggy shrugged and said she couldn't remember. Cassius Fletcher wagged his tail hopefully. He wanted to get down on the floor to stretch his legs. 'You'd better trim him to about an inch all over,' said Alison. 'Pity you cut his beard off though.'

'It'll grow,' said Peggy automatically. This was the stock answer we gave to the owners of our mistakes – the dogs that we had sometimes pared to the bone in our enthusiasm to test our new-found skills. But as it turned out Mrs Fletcher was delighted with her streamlined Cassius and said that from now on she would bring him in regularly for his short back and sides.

All this and much more I mulled over as the Paddington to Exeter train bore me homewards. I was dying for someone to come up to me with a doggy problem to be solved – a skin rash perhaps, for now I knew the difference between mange and eczema and if it was eczema how to diagnose the probable cause. In addition I could clean ears, scale teeth, clip claws and even, if pushed, empty anal glands. But nobody noticed the latter-day St Francis in their midst or admired the shiny new canine beautician's case which I had placed ostentatiously on the empty seat beside me. It reminded me of the time I first became a Tail Wagger at the age of eight. Tail Waggers wore badges to inform the world that here were people who did doggy good deeds but then, as now, the world didn't notice. Actually some did. Angry owners of 'strays' I persistently kidnapped on Hampstead Heath and took to the police station would implore the local constabulary to 'do something about that bloody kid with the badge'.

It was good to be sitting down on a comfortable seat at ten in the morning. I guessed it would be quite a while before such a treat came my way again and certainly there wouldn't be men in pretty red jackets to keep me topped up with coffee at home.

Chapter Two

'HOME' WAS NOW a nasty place. It was a 1930s bungalow that would have been nasty in any circumstances but compared to our last place – a beautiful thatched Tudor farmhouse – it was even more of an outrage. From the outside it resembled one of those prewar beach chalets that people used to rent in east-coast resorts. Inside it was mournful; an unloved house, designed by someone with no sense of texture or proportion and so damp it gave off a soggy smell like a marsh.

We had bought it because it went with the latest project – a derelict nursery/market garden situated in five south-facing Devon acres. Our goal was to resurrect the site and establish a viable (and saleable) business as quickly as possible and, to this end, we had sold our farm and all the stock except the pets and invested the capital in this daunting heap. We don't daunt easily but after a few weeks in the damp ugly bungalow our spirits had sunk deep into our wellies. Then Anne, my mother, had generously offered to pay for me to go away for the dog-grooming course so that a) it would cheer me up and b) we would have another means of earning some money while we were setting up the new premises.

I got back from the course on December 21st, the shortest day and one which, curiously, always puts us in a good mood. You know that whatever else may happen the days *will* get longer, and snowdrops and primroses will soon come up and show the flag. Brian was waiting for me at Exeter station looking surprisingly well – cold nose, the lot. 'I've ordered a Chinese take-away,' he said, banging the van doors shut on my suitcases. 'We can collect it on the way back.'

Gosh, the relief. What a lovely homecoming. I had not been looking forward to a defrosted dog dinner. (What an idiot I'd been to put D for dog and H for human on the frozen meals. Brian had assumed D meant dinner for him and H meant Honey.)

He had made good progress with the site clearance while I had been away but now, with Christmas just a few days away, he downed tools and together we whizzed round shops in a last-minute frenzy of present-buying. Our children Marcus and Sara would be tearing themselves away from their with-it London friends and had promised us three whole days of their company. My mother would complete the gathering but had taken one look at the condensation running down the bedroom walls and elected to be a day-girl rather than a boarder. She now lived on the banks of the River Dart, in a lovely cottage, part of which had been used for paper-making by some twelfth-century monks.

When Marcus and Sara first saw the bungalow we were treated to a non-stop barrage of jokes along the lines of 'Why don't you blow it down and start again' and 'Good job we bought you three plaster ducks for Christmas.' But when Marcus went into the conservatory – a glazed extension built on to the west wall of the house – inspiration dried up and he could only lean weakly against the crimson and gold flocked wallpaper and gulp.

'Brothel?' Sara suggested.

'No, too hot in summer. Indian restaurant or tenth-rate night club more like.' He picked experimentally at the three-dimensional wallpaper.

'Don't make it worse,' I said. 'We won't have time to decorate in here for ages. Come and see the sitting-room carpet.'

The sitting room was large and sunny and was fitted with a carpet that was a swirling spectrum – purple and orange, yellow, red, green and pink, all woven together to produce a sort of instant vertigo. 'I must sit down before I fall down,' Sara said. 'Can't you cover it up with sacks or something?'

'You two are getting brain rot in your old age,' said Marcus, sinking down on to the settee. 'You didn't *buy* it, did you? It looks brand new.'

Brian laughed. 'It came with the house,' he said. 'The last people emigrated.' We all stared at the carpet in silence for a while. The log fire crackled cheerfully but it couldn't compete with the psychedelic acres. Marcus nudged Sara. 'I spy with my little eye,' he said, 'something beginning with G.'

'Gnomes,' said Sara promptly. 'There are bound to be gnomes here.'

'There were,' Brian said, 'but we shot most of them on moving day.' (Moving day had not gone quite as smoothly as usual. It had rained non-stop and the tractor had fallen through the floor of one of the removal vans, so to cheer things along a bit we had lined the gnomes up on a wall and invited the removal men to try their skill with an air rifle.)

'We saved some for you to shoot,' I said. 'Some real horrors – fishing off toadstools and worse.' Sara said there was nothing like an old-fashioned family Christmas, was there, and what had Marcus seen beginning with G?

'The grate,' Marcus said. 'No wonder they emigrated. It's shell-shaped.'

Shell-shocked would have been a better description. The scalloped edges of the grate protruded from an imitation marble fireplace of unbelievably bad design, worse than the Albert Memorial. It only needed seaside souvenirs in each of its many nooks and crannies to make it the classic 1930s Yuck period piece.

None of us could think of anything that would improve the fireplace but we did manage to solve the problem of the rainbow carpet: we used it as an underlay for an old one of our own. A shaggy hearthrug was then thrown down to challenge the gruesome fireplace and straight away the room became more friendly. It would always be a prickly house though because it was so badly made – flat roof, metal windows and so forth – but we were sure that a few gallons of white paint and a fairly free hand with a crowbar would improve things.

Christmas was spent quietly, taking the dogs for walks on Dartmoor (unexplored territory for us), playing cards, shooting the rest of the gnomes and having drinks with our neighbours, Bunty and Gordon. They were a very nice early-retired couple whose beautiful thatched cottage lay just beyond our paddock. They had their grown-up children staying for Christmas too, a wholesome trio who did normal things like passing exams and providing Bunty and Gordon with grandchildren. We were never quite sure what ours did; they seemed to be part of an alternative society where jobs, bedsits and partners were ever changing. Whatever it was they were doing they did it three hundred miles away which was something to be thankful for.

Once Christmas was out of the way we ran out of excuses for not getting on with the clearing of the site. The whole nursery had suffered appalling snow damage during the previous arctic winter but the main job was to dismantle and remove the biggest of the glasshouses which was broken beyond repair. It was a five-span (M-shaped) house extending to about a third of an acre. The weight of the snow in the dip of the M had buckled all the girders and pulled the four sides of the house inwards where they now rested at a dangerous 45° angle. Lethal-looking daggers of broken glass stuck out everywhere.

'We'll take a ladder each,' Brian said, 'and start unbolting the overhead lights.'

Plainly he was under the impression that he was married to a gang of Irish navvies. 'Lights' in horticultural parlance has nothing to do with illumination. A light is a wooden frame usually about 6' by 3' with a cross-strut across the middle and glazed with heavy-duty glass.

'You're potty,' I said. 'I can't hold one of those above my head.'

'Yes you can. They're not all that heavy. Put your step-ladder down there parallel with mine and we'll do an end each.' He scrunched through a sea of broken glass and climbed to the top of his ladder. It wobbled.

'It's wobbling,' I said, playing for time. He took no notice but fished a shifting spanner and a pair of pliers out of his pocket. I looked in my tool bag. It contained a shifting spanner and a pair of pliers. 'OK, I give in,' I said and climbed my ladder. 'What do I do now?'

'Hold the bolts firm with the pliers and loosen the nuts with the spanner. I've given everything a squirt of easing oil so they should come off.'

Drawing a thirty-six inch tapeworm from the anus of a friend's pig comes quite high on the list of things I would prefer not to do again. However, swaying around on a step-ladder in January sleet loosening rusty bolts is a lot worse. It was bad enough when the bolts were reachable but the ones that were fifteen feet above ground level presented quite a challenge to a 5'4" person standing on an 8' ladder.

'Can't you reach?' Brian called. 'Here, pull the girder down towards you.' He hung like a chimpanzee from a roof girder and a pane of glass slid down and splintered on to the ground. Brian said the retaining nails must have been rusty. He loosened the six bolts at his end, then changed places with me on my ladder and did mine. 'Carefully does it,' he said. 'Throw the bolts into a bucket and lower your end a bit at a time.'

After dismantling three more lights we had to stop for a breather because our eyes and mouths were full of rust. I thought I was doing quite well as a scrap-man's mate until Brian pointed to the bucketful of bolts and asked where the nuts were.

'Nuts?' I said.

'Yes, nuts. What's the good of a bolt without a nut?'

Gosh, what a lot of gaps there were in my education. Bolts, it seemed, needed nuts just as Marks needed Spencer and fish needed chips. 'Sorry,' I said. 'I just let them drop when I unscrewed the other end. What do you want hundreds of bolts for anyway?'

'To make things with of course. They're terribly expensive to buy new.'

(Five years on we still have enough six-inch and four-inch bolts to reassemble the Eiffel Tower and the cat's box is so strongly made she must think she's a lion.)

'OK, I'll keep them together after this. Horrible job, isn't it?'

'Mm. What we need is goggles to stop the rust getting in our eyes.' To our great surprise the next post brought us two pairs of old-fashioned motorcycling goggles. A friend of ours called Ian, a great do-it-yourselfer whose home is a Professor Branestawm maze of mechanical inventions, had heard of our

19

struggles with the girders and sent the sort of help he knew from experience was needed.

So, suitably protected round the eyes and with scarves over our mouths, we carried on demolishing – a mindless conveyor-belt routine of wrench-twist-twiddle, and *crash* into the bucket, on and on, day after day.

A fortnight later only one roof section remained. Ice and light snow covered the site and we were frozen stiff. 'I can finish this off,' Brian said. 'You go and make some coffee.' I went thankfully indoors and put the kettle on. A moment later Brian hurried in and went straight to the sink. 'I've cut my hand,' he said calmly, and ran the cold tap. 'Get the car out, would you?'

'The plasters are in— ' I caught sight of his hand. *Hells bells.* Pulling open a kitchen drawer I took out all the clean tea towels and thrust them into his good hand before rushing outside to turn the car round. I opened the passenger door and he got in, holding his arm up as high as he could. Blood was pumping out of his hand and running down his sleeve. He clamped a tea towel over the wound. 'There's a sign for a hospital outside the next village,' he said. 'Let's try there.'

I drove like the clappers, amazed at his calmness. He's hopeless at cat-sick or afterbirth. Perhaps blood was different, perhaps he had lost so much he was getting lightheaded . . . 'Shall I open a window?' I said.

'No, I'm OK. Just drive.'

'What blood group are you?'

'O positive.'

'Are you? So am I.' It did seem a strange conversation, as if we had only just met. 'I'll be able to give you some then if you need it.'

After a few miles we found ourselves in the courtyard of a small cottage hospital on the outskirts of a village. In the reception area some old ladies were making practice runs on walking frames. They stopped as Brian dripped in and one of them called: 'Nu . . . rse – customer for you.' Then they made a sort of guard of honour with their frames so that we could squeeze past. A Sister appeared, took in the situation in a flash, and whipped Brian into a side room.

I was left to wait with the old ladies who, I learned, had all had falls on icy pavements and were being taught how to cope with plastered legs before being sent home. It was a lovely hospital, they said, warm and friendly and not too big. 'Mind you,' one of them added, 'if your hubby needs stitches he'll have to go to Exeter. You can't get stitches here.'

'And you can thank the sodding Tories for that,' put in another. I stared at her. Surely even the sodding Tories weren't rationing stitches?

'He does need stitches,' I said. 'He's cut an artery.'

'You didn't vote for them, did you?' said the anti-Tory old lady accusingly.

'No, of course not. I vote for the Ecology person if there is one, otherwise I don't vote at all.' This didn't go down too well. I ought to vote Labour, they said, not that Labour had been the same since poor Mr Gaitskell died . . . Then Brian came back with the Sister who was looking very cheerful. 'Your husband's going to get me some early salpiglossis,' she beamed.

I looked at Brian crossly. 'Can't you *ever* do one thing at a time? You're supposed to be bleeding to death, not mixing business with pleasure.'

'Pleasure? You call being cut to the bone pleasure?' He held his bandaged finger aloft.

'It's very deep,' confirmed his new friend, 'and it needs stitching. I've stopped the bleeding but I'm afraid you'll have to take him to Exeter straight away.'

'You haven't stitched it then?' I said, avoiding looking at the old ladies who were making 'we told you so' noises.

'It's the National Health cutbacks,' Brian explained. 'They haven't got a resident doctor here so there's nobody qualified to stitch. Come on, let's go to Exeter.'

'Exeter's got cutbacks too,' the old ladies' spokesman said darkly. 'My neighbour went there to get sterilised and she came back pregnant.'

'*Mrs Benson*,' said the Sister in exasperation. 'Your neighbour was sent home because she was found to be *already* pregnant – she didn't get pregnant at the hospital. I do wish you would get your facts right.'

21

'She wasn't pregnant when her husband was working,' retorted Mrs Benson, skilfully bringing her argument full circle, 'and if that cow in Number 10 hadn't made him redundant he wouldn't have been under her feet all day, would he?'

Good-humouredly the Sister conceded game set and match to Mrs Benson and saw us to the door. 'Mind how you go,' she said. 'I don't want any more fracture cases this winter.'

We drove to the next hospital. Brian was taken away to be sewn up and came back some time later looking less than chirpy. The reason for this, I learned on the drive home, was because he had seen his own bones. He hadn't meant to look but the young houseman's enthusiasm for a stitching job after endless fractures was catching, and when he had said 'Look at that' Brian had looked. I was envious.

'You are lucky,' I said. 'I've never seen a live bone.'

'That was the awful bit,' Brian said. 'It didn't look at all live. It was more like blanched celery – quite colourless.'

'What about the ligament and muscles?' I prompted, but prudishly he didn't want to talk about what went on under his skin.

The cut took ages to heal up. It was in an awkward place between the thumb and forefinger and the healing process was not exactly aided by his stubbornly getting back to work too soon. The doctor had told him to rest the hand but Brian interpreted 'rest' rather loosely and treated the injury to a mere two days' holiday. Within a week he had split all the stitches and had to have six fresh ones put in. The hospital staff were marvellous, changing his earthstained, bloodstained dressing every second day and commiserating with him about the need to get the site clearance finished before the spring. He got no sympathy from me however because he wouldn't drink the herbal remedies I brewed up for him and hell hath no fury like a woman whose comfrey tea has been spurned.

The weather continued to be cold. One particularly foul day our neighbours Gordon and Bunty asked us if we would like to go to the pictures with them that evening. 'Not exactly with us,' Gordon said. 'We're taking some friends in our car but you can follow. Bring a torch.' It seemed that three other cars would be in the convoy too, so, rather mystified as to why everyone in the neighbourhood wanted to go to the pictures on the same night and why we needed a torch, we said yes.

Our Transit van having chosen honourable death in a breaker's yard to life as our slave, we were now the proud owners of a minivan. It cost £225 and in the five years we had it, it never cost us a penny in repairs other than replacement tyres. Obviously for £225 it didn't have a perfect body; in wet weather rain came in through the roof and in mud or slush the stuff simply oozed through holes in the floor. But it *went* and that's really all that matters in the country.

On the night of the cinema outing we prepared three hot-water bottles – one each for us and one in case the radiator leaked – donned wellingtons and set off. Gordon's car went first, then three others, then us bringing up the rear. When we got to the main road the convoy didn't head towards town as we expected but in the opposite direction, towards Dartmoor.

'Where on earth is he going?' said Brian, peering through the sleet at the tail-lights of the car ahead. 'This road doesn't lead anywhere.'

What he meant was it didn't lead anywhere that could possibly have a cinema. And he was right. The road led to Dartmoor itself, up narrow lanes so steep we had to use first gear and where outwintered sheep, ponies and cattle stood with their backs to the snow flurries, oblivious of our cars skirting round them. After going six miles, during which time we didn't see a house or a light, we followed the frontrunners into the courtyard of a small pub. Gordon came over grinning broadly. 'Did you enjoy the drive? Bet you've never been to a cinema like this before?'

'Gordon, where are we?' I said, struggling out of my wellingtons in the cramped confines of the passenger seat. Gordon shone his torch into the van and politely didn't ask why the floor was awash. 'It's a pub,' he said, 'and once a fortnight it's a cinema too. We're having Agatha Christie and risotto tonight. Don't forget to cover your windscreen or it'll ice up.' He rejoined Bunty and their friends. Brian and I changed into shoes, shook some of the water out of our hair, then followed everyone in to the bar. Soon drinks were circulating and there was a nice matey atmosphere. Someone asked us if we had walked and Brian said no we had had the sun roof open and what was all this about risotto?

'Oh, you get supper at half-time. It's all included in the price of the ticket.'

As the tickets were only 60p we wondered what sort of refreshment could possibly be included. At eight o'clock a bell rang and everybody left the bar and filed in to another room where rows of chairs had been set out facing a white screen. 'Don't sit at the back,' Bunty warned. 'The projectionist has got a cold.'

The film was Agatha Christie's *Death on the Nile* which I believe was showing at the Leicester Square Odeon about that time. Our cinema may not have had all the comforts of the Leicester Square Odeon – there was no heating, for instance – but it was unbeatable for rustic charm. Silhouettes of the pub's kitchen staff were clearly visible on the screen alongside Peter Ustinov as Poirot and their conversation filled in any silences on the official soundtrack. They were talking about the infant school's Nativity play: ''Tweren't fair. He'd bin *promised* he could be one of the wise men on account of him going up into juniors next year . . .'

Peter Ustinov was on a white ship now. Sparkling blue water and bright sunshine brought forth oohs of appreciation from the Dartmoor-wintering audience and someone observed loudly that he could have done with some of that sun for his hay last year. The projectionist, who should have been in bed with Vick on his chest, blew his nose. Another member of the audience called out: 'Turn the volume up a bit, mister.'

Agatha Christie's characters divided themselves into murder victims and suspects and the story, with a few stops for the reels to be changed, unfolded. Poirot spent quite a lot of time in quiet contemplation so we were able to pay full attention to the continuing grievances of the kitchen lady whose six-year-old son had failed to land a plum part in his school play. On the face of it, it did seem a little unfair that her Jonathan should have had to make do with being a

shepherd while all three of the Wise Men had only landed their parts after remedial reading lessons. Jonathan's mother's confidante who evidently hadn't got a child in the infants dismissed the entire Nativity play as a waste of time and with Agate-like ferocity concluded: 'And that Tracy Blackstock's Mary weren't nothing to write home about neither. It were as plain as plain she were going to shed her milk teeth before the first night.'

Whether this meant the aggrieved shepherd had actually helped Tracy Blackstock's wobbling teeth out we never discovered as the landlord came in then and switched the lights on. 'Risotto, ladies and gents,' he announced. 'Stay in your seats, please.'

The risotto, nicely cooked and piping hot, was dished out in large china soup bowls and passed along the rows until everybody was served. It was most welcome as by now the audience was looking pinched with cold. Coffee followed, also served in china crockery. All this for 60p a head – the Leicester Square Odeon just wasn't in the same league.

After everyone had finished, the bronchial projectionist restarted the film and it became apparent that there was a minor flaw in the Management's otherwise excellent arrangements. The noise of the china and cutlery being washed up, dried and stacked quite upstaged Peter Ustinov and Co and reduced the behind-the-screen dialogue to a few tantalising snatches.

But eventually the kitchen staff went home, leaving us to pick up the threads of the story and to work out who were the goodies and who were the baddies. Poirot solved his case and tidied up the sub-plots, then the projector stopped whirring and the lights came on again.

There was a stampede to the bar to get warming drinks before closing time. These were not included in the ticket price and the pub did a brisk trade for the last half hour which was fair enough as there couldn't have been any profit in the film and supper. There was coffee too for people who were driving and an invitation from the landlord to come again. Next time, he said, it would be James Bond and chicken and chips.

Chapter Three

IT HAD BEEN kind of Gordon and Bunty to include us in the visit to what must surely rate as one of the most unusual establishments showing *Death on the Nile*. We repaid their kindness by accidentally cutting off the water supply to their house a few days later.

Gordon, never having been a smallholder, is the sort of man who worries if he turns on a tap and nothing happens. He phoned us: 'I say Brian, is your water all right?'

'Yes, it's fine. We had it analysed before we moved in.'

'No, actually I didn't mean the purity – I meant have you got any? Could you try your taps? I'll hang on.'

Brian tried the taps and went back to the phone: 'Gushing out,' he reported.

'Oh, gushing, is it? Does it normally gush?'

Brian admitted that gravity-fed well water seldom gushed and that we did seem to have more than usual.

'Well, I'm sorry, Brian, but I think you must have ours. We haven't got a drop. I'd better come over.' Like a schoolboy asking for his ball back Gordon came round to our garden to retrieve his lost water.

Together we explored the complexities of a shared water supply which was not unlike a telephone party-line in that one of the parties could, and manifestly had, cut the other one off. Happily the guilt had to be shared – between Brian and myself – since neither could remember which of us had altered the relevant stop-cock, so divorce proceedings were suspended once more. Bunty, stationed at their kitchen tap, phoned with the good news that after a lot of banging in the pipe the water was now coming through and how about some coffee?

Good neighbourliness is not only a pleasant state of affairs but in the country, where weed seeds leave home when you're not looking or someone's axle may break on the very day guests have to be met at the station, it can be an aid to survival. With Gordon and Bunty we tried extra hard, especially in the weed and pony control department. We felt guilty that we had the benefit of overlooking their marvellous garden and period cottage while our ghastly bungalow was part of their view. In the two and a half years that we were neighbours there were only two occasions when Bunty had to ask us to get our ponies off their lawn ('Faith dear, we like ponies but . . .'), a statistic that never fails to impress fellow pony-owners. I think it says a lot for the reliability of electric fencing.

The weeks galloped by the way they do when you don't want them to and soon it was time to start sowing seeds. Apart from the wrecked glasshouse there were two others, a ninety-foot long Alumabrite and a hundred foot propagating house, both in working order. As with any project involving plants (or animals) the houses had to be disinfected before introducing fresh stock. Gallons of Jeyes Fluid were brushed and sprayed over every visible inch and awful-smelling smoke bombs lit inside to take care of any bugs lurking in the cracks.

Brian sowed a wide variety of seeds in electrically heated boxes which he had made earlier in the winter, boxes that worked like a dream and germinated tray after tray of healthy-looking seedlings. I couldn't get over it – I'm always impressed when technology works – and kept nipping in to the propagating house to admire the new little plants. Brian threatened to padlock the door if I didn't keep out because I was upsetting his humidity every time I let the cold air in.

'You'll check their growth,' he said, guarding the trays like a tigress with cubs. 'They won't be even.'

I had read enough back numbers of *Grower* magazine to know that uneven growth is a capital offence in commercial horticulture so I rationed my visits to two a day.

And goodness knows there were enough other things to do. Nasty jobs like washing thousands of second-hand flowerpots – in *cold* water, God it was awful – nice ones like bonfires, and average ones. Shovelling barrowloads of broken glass was an average job at first, then the glass mountain grew so big we were having to fling the stuff to the top, so that became as unpopular as washing pots. A scrap-dealer called Alf Paris who had been following our progress with the site was an invaluable help during this period, taking away anything that couldn't be burnt or recycled, but even he drew the line at broken glass.

The pace hotted up even if the weather didn't. A thousand geranium cuttings were delivered and, being unrooted, had to be planted immediately. My admiration for Brian's heated boxes was nothing compared to my amazement when I first saw our mist propagation unit in action. It consisted of a 20' by 5' sand tray at table-top height inside a polythene tent. You plant unrooted cuttings straight into the damp sand (it was rather like being back at playgroup) and secure the sides of the tent to the sides of the tray. Thermostatically controlled networks of wire under the sand ensure that the cuttings stay at the right temperature, but the magical bit is how the unit waters or 'mists' itself. Imitation plants made out of paper-thin metal are placed among the cuttings and electronic sensors in their leaves measure the amount of moisture inside the tent. As soon as a metal leaf gets dry it automatically triggers off a fine spray of water all over the real plants, then switches itself off a few seconds later.

We watched over our geranium cuttings like parents of premature babies, opening the door carefully and fiddling with the sides of the tent if it looked as though a draught of non-humidified air might get in. And they grew apace in their jungly atmosphere. There were a few losses: the ones that we kept pulling up to see if they were alive . . .

In the Alumabrite, the cold greenhouse, we planted two hundred sweetpea seedlings to get an early cut-flower crop and Brian sowed a few rows of outdoor sweetpeas as a follow-on crop. Container-grown shrubs were delivered by the lorry-load, as were conifers, heathers, alpines, hardy perennials and roses. The roses were a mistake. They cost us £1.50 each wholesale and were no better than the ones Woolworth's were retailing at 99p each.

On the whole though we were pleased with the quality of

the bought-in stock. Buying from wholesalers chosen at random from trade journals and catalogues could have been a gamble but either we were lucky or else all horticultural wholesalers tend to be honest. They were lazy about labelling, however, supplying only one labelled plant of each variety in every batch and leaving the retailer to duplicate the information himself. This didn't matter too much if it was something like Hosta but copying out Viburnum Rhytidophyllum fifty times on small plastic ties could get tedious and in cases like Cotoneaster Franchetii Sternianus was well-nigh impossible.

Brian couldn't write small enough to do the labels so I had that dubious honour. He helped by sorting out the plants into species – the lorry drivers unloaded them in no particular order – and calling out how many of what I had to label.

'Thirty-five Chamaecyparis Lawsoniana,' he would say.

'How do you spell it?'

He would spell it out and go on to the next lot: 'Thirty-five Chamaecyparis Ellwoodii. Don't get these confused with Nootkatensis, will you?'

'Why not?'

'One's a dwarf and one grows to over thirty feet.'

'I'll put the labels on the lowest branches to be on the safe side.' And I would write the names on a clip-board then go indoors to write the labels in the warmth of the kitchen. I grew to detest people who have plants named after them because I had to cramp their silly names – all ending in double 'i' for some reason – on to the label alongside the botanical name. Hebe Variegata would have been a piece of cake if someone called Anderson hadn't got in on the act and made me write Hebe Andersonii Variegata one hundred times. I even took against some *plants* if their names had given me trouble; in particular the Euonymus which I thought I could spell without looking it up and found out too late that I couldn't.

The final resting place (but not too final we hoped) of the stock was to be in enclosed sand beds on the site of the fast-vanishing old glasshouse. Alf Paris was ferrying away scrap metal and giving us ten pounds a ton for it and gradually foundations were revealing themselves. It had been a very large house – a third of an acre – so there were plenty of beds all neatly intersected by concrete paths in good condition.

Brian ordered twenty tons of silver sand and a gigantic roll of heavy-duty black polythene. The idea was to cut the polythene into oblong strips, line the old beds with it, then fill in each bed with sand. The reason for the polythene was first to stop weeds growing up into the display beds and secondly to retain moisture at root level. In principle, lining the beds was no harder than lining a pie dish with pastry and, in fact, if it hadn't been for the wind we could have done it in no time. But the weather was squally and the immense strips of polythene each about 30′ by 3′ caught the wind and tugged us about like hang-gliders. We needed something to hold the middle down, not rocks or the polythene would split but something soft and fat and heavy.

As I sat in the display bed giving a passable imitation of a garden gnome, it did cross my mind that there must be more to life than being human ballast.

'You OK?' Brian called.

'Yes thank you. I love sitting out in a howling gale having wet sand tipped over me.'

'You can move now if you want to. I've put enough sand on the corners to hold it down while we get some more. Have the aluminium barrow – it's lighter,' he added generously.

When it was filled with sand the aluminium barrow was marginally lighter than Mount Everest. 'Hey,' said Brian, 'don't fill it right up or you'll hurt your back.'

But even with the barrows half filled we both managed to hurt our backs and looking through our cheque stubs later in the year were amused to find that we had spent almost as much on osteopath's fees as on silver sand. It wasn't too funny at the time though and I vowed to spend my next incarnation as an earthworm (no spine) while Brian opted for being a swan on the Thames. Meanwhile, our more immediate goal was in sight – all the display beds were finished.

We were so proud of them we wanted to photograph them before they became dirty with use but as it was always raining the sparkly effect of sunshine on silver sand had to be left to the viewer's imagination. If there is ever a competition for the dullest picture, our study of 'empty sand beds in the rain' would probably get the prize.

Setting out the container-grown stock in the beds, it soon became painfully obvious that we didn't have enough. There were sixty varieties of shrubs – between thirty and a hundred of each – about thirty kinds of conifers in ditto numbers, thousands of alpines and five hundred assorted roses and climbers. In the fruit section there were just ten varieties, from gooseberries to currants. This little lot had cost four thousands pounds, not nearly enough to stock a Garden Centre but it was all we had.

'Never mind,' I said. 'It'll look more when it grows. When shall we open?'

'How about May 1st? That gives us five weeks to finish the site and put up some polytunnels.'

The end of March was enlivened by the arrival of a firm of builders, called in to replace part of the bungalow roof which had blown away in the spring gales. It seemed a straightforward enough job and the boss, a very friendly and helpful man, said he would put a couple of young chaps on it who were used to flat-roof work. The young chaps duly arrived and the countryside rang with Radio 1 noise accompanied by light hammering. A smart perspex dome rose out of the roof – this was our new bathroom skylight replacement for the one that blew away – giving the bungalow a somewhat spaceship appearance.

But whether it was the impact of Radio 1 or the ravages of wind and weather, the roof itself developed other problems and the rain came in worse than ever. Brian sent off a claim to the National Farmers Union who were our insurers at that time and they refused to pay. The building firm boss said he wasn't a bit surprised as in his experience the NFU were lousy insurers and why didn't we switch to Eagle Star? Meanwhile he called in an arbitrator who found in our favour and made the NFU pay the bill. While all this paperwork was going on our two unmusical friends had made themselves comfortable on the roof and in the weeks they were up there – they could only work on fine days – became almost part of the family. They brought their own tea things at first but soon realised it was coals to Newcastle in a household where tea was served in large mugs six times a day. They were so happy sloshing barrels of molten tar over the roof I hardly liked to spoil their fun but one day I had to.

'Steve, John,' I called. 'Could you come down for a minute?'

Two heads appeared, flanking a downpipe like gargoyles. 'Anything wrong, Mrs A?'

'There's tar running down the kitchen walls. Come and look.'

They climbed down their ladder and trod tar prints into the kitchen. 'Oops sorry,' said Steve. 'Forgot you had a carpet in here.'

'Never mind the carpet,' I said. (Like everything else in the house it was expendable.) 'It's the walls I'm worried about. That's tar, isn't it?'

The lads peered closely at the tar as if they hadn't seen tar before. 'It looks like tar,' they admitted.

'It *is* tar,' I said. 'I thought you were supposed to be tarring the roof. What's it doing in here?'

'It's come in through the cracks in the roof,' Steve explained. 'Look there's some more starting in the ceiling.' We watched a droplet of tar form in the middle of the ceiling. I put a cloth under it before it fell.

'How long is this going on for?' I asked. 'We can't have the place streaming with tar.'

'It's better than having it streaming with water, Mrs A,' said Steve, 'and it'll pick off easy enough when it's dry.' Having promised to try to make the next barrel of tar less runny they returned to their perches.

The kitchen decor was such that having tarred walls was almost an improvement. There hadn't been time to do any decorating since we moved in and the walls were still aggressively red, white and blue. The dogs were doing their best to camouflage the carpet with pawmarks but even in wet weather it was taking a long time.

*

Spring brought city friends out of hibernation for weekend visits. Sue and Keith and family, who had put me up during the dog beauticians' course, were among the first and were a great help with all the transplanting that needed to be done. As well as the seedlings he had grown Brian also bought boxes of bedding-plant seedlings from other nurseries so that we would have a wide selection to sell. The seedlings, five hundred to a thousand in a box, had to be transplanted or pricked out into trays of twelve, then put to one side for a few weeks to harden off. It was an enjoyable job and all the more so if there was a crowd of you doing it.

The four of us sat up at the propagation-house benches on tall stools, planting alyssum, lobelia, mesembryanthemum and all the other popular bedding stock. Lauren, who had got up to W in the alphabet, 'wrote' labels. She wrote W on all of them and I can never now see a capital W without recalling her earnest three-year-old voice repeating: 'All the way down and all the way up then all the way down again and all the way up again.' Not to be outshone by his clever elder sister, Jordan did some creative work with half a bucket of cold tar the builders had left at ground level. When we found him his expression was one of pure bliss. Sue's expression was quite different and they didn't come again for ages.

Another, longer-term visitor was Magnus, a young magpie. One morning we were woken up by what sounded like somebody typing in the garden.

'Are we expecting anyone?' Brian said.

'Only the builders. And only if it isn't raining.' We lay there for a while trying to guess who could possibly be typing in the back garden at seven a.m. Maybe the builders were writing a bestseller while they waited for their tar to cool down. Unable to bear the suspense we got up and opened the curtains a crack. There, on the rockery, was a family of magpies – mother, father and a bedraggled looking fledgling. The youngster was standing in the bird bath and it was the clackety clack of his flapping wings that was making the typewriter noise.

'He's stuck,' I said.

'How can he be stuck in half an inch of water? All he's got

to do is hop out.' We watched for a bit longer, then when it was obvious that the fledgling was in difficulties went outside to fish him out. The parent birds flew up on to the fence but came back again directly we had rescued their sodden offspring and put him on the grass to dry.

As the days passed and we got to know Magnus, as we called him, we realised that nearly drowning in half an inch of water was just the sort of thing that would happen to him. He was a clueless bird entirely dependent on miracles to keep him out of danger – miracles like Small our cat taking a scientific rather than gastronomic interest in him. By cat standards she is minute and a young magpie looks surprisingly big close up. At any rate, she wasn't taking any chances and Magnus, far from regarding her as a natural enemy, would actually hop towards her if he saw her spying on him in the undergrowth.

His conscientious parents kept a twenty-four hour vigil over him and a fast-food service going during daylight hours. They tried to teach him how to preen his feathers but he was either too dim or too idle to copy them and his plumage remained dull and spiky. Birds need clean feathers in order to fly, so naturally Magnus's dishevelled appearance effectively grounded him. He was the original bird-brain.

At length – I think it was about ten days after his typing impersonation – Magnus's parents decided that enough was enough and flew away. Magnus was devastated. I was putting some rubbish in the dustbin when this traumatic event occurred and stayed outside for a while to see how he would cope.

He called and hopped up and down in a fine old paddy. Nothing happened, no food, no parents – nothing. He turned the volume up. Still nothing.

'Eat the bread on the ground, idiot,' I told him. But of course he didn't know how to, his mother had always put it in his beak for him. Hearing my voice he turned towards me and gaped for food. If he had been really incapable I would have helped him but I have never had the slightest desire to take on someone else's teenage reject and certainly not a punk magpie. 'No way, boy,' I said to him. 'You're on your own.' And I went indoors.

Some hours later, when we were checking up on the ponies for the night, we found him perched on Noah's back. We guessed he must have got on when Noah was lying down and clung on when he rose to his feet. Since neither pony seemed to mind their new charge we left them to it and for the whole of that summer Magnus grew up as a pony, sharing their food (recycled), water and shelter. He rode on their backs, sometimes experimentally tugging at their hair and always cawing away in his hoarse monotonous voice. Eventually he taught himself to fly but each evening came home to roost with his adopted guardians. I wish we had had the time to do a Lorenz-type study of their relationship but as with a lot of projects it had to be shelved while we got on with the less interesting but rather more pressing job of earning a living.

May started with a bang, an ear-shattering thunderstorm followed by heavy rain. Our Grand Opening was not very grand at all, just a lot of splashing through puddles to serve the handful of customers who braved the weather to come and see what the new Garden Centre had to offer. People who stroll round garden centres in pouring rain are always fanatically keen gardeners and as such are easy to serve. They know the botanical and common names of all the plants they're after so you don't have to waste hours thumbing through reference books for them.

At the end of the first day there was only forty pounds in the cash box but we were pleased that everything had gone smoothly and that our customers had been complimentary about the stock. It had been a long time since we had served in a shop and in a masochistic sort of way it was nice being back in harness. My personal nightmare about shopkeeping during our London flowershop days used to be adding up prices and giving the right change so, to prevent a recurrence of the time in pre-decimal days when I thought there were ten half-crowns to the pound, Brian priced all the plants in multiples of five pence. This helped considerably – even I can add up in fives, provided there aren't too many of them – and Brian also invested 15p on a ready reckoner for me in case I got a big spender. This was just as well because a spell of sunny weather brought crowds of customers and trade was so brisk that at the end of some days there were just imprints of pots in the display beds where the plants had stood and we had to rearrange the remaining stock to hide the gaps. Brian spent every possible minute in the greenhouses, potting on replacement bedding plants and only coming over to the selling area if he saw a queue building up.

We were open seven days a week from dawn till dusk but as we had to have time off to eat we left the shop unattended at meal times and provided a cowbell for customers to ring for service if they couldn't find what they were looking for. Usually they could and they would bring their money to the kitchen door and apologise for interrupting our meal. Some people felt so guilty about disturbing us they would simply leave the money in the selling area weighted down with a stone. Others, more security conscious, would hide the money and leave cryptic notes: 'Have taken 6 Mustang. Money Iceberg.' Being crossword enthusiasts we had no difficulty with most clues but one or two floored us: '2 red-hot pokers – money you know where' for example. Where, conceivably, would a person put red-hot poker money? It was only when Brian was looking something up in a reference book (we kept about twelve in the shop) and three pound notes fluttered out that he realised that the red-hot poker customer had tucked it into the book under the proper name of Kniphofia.

They kept us on our toes, our free-ranging, knowledge-seeking, sometimes money-spending customers. We nicknamed the regulars: Pink Anorak, Big Feet, Isadora Duncan, Nice Day and so on. There was one – Lady Muck we called her – who was so horrible we would both find urgent jobs to do if she appeared and hope she would get tired of waiting. She was a patronising old trout – sixtyish, small and dark – and drove a Range Rover. The first time she came she said she was looking for something to give as a get-well present. Brian showed her some easy-going plants which are always a safe bet if you don't know the recipient's soil type but she kept rejecting them and moving along the beds.

'What sort of thing have you got in mind?' Brian asked patiently. 'A climber, evergreen, alpine?'

'Something cheap,' snapped Lady Muck. 'It's only for my charwoman.'

After a lot of deliberating she eventually bought a 25p-primula and Brian had to have three sugars in his tea to calm himself down.

After that we saw her quite often, not only at our place but in local shops. She liked to tell anyone within earshot the story of her life; how that wretched government had compulsorily purchased her father's estate and built Crawley new town all over the best pasture. How the family had never got over the disgrace and had fled to the West Country to pig it (in a manor house the size of Hampton Court) and how you couldn't keep staff nowadays. There was no Lord Muck, just labradors.

Another customer, fortunately a one-off, was a North Country man on business in Devon and wanting to buy some heathers to take home. I directed him to the heather bed and was going to leave him to browse when suddenly he stopped and pointed to something among the plants. 'Is that your bee?' he said accusingly.

'My what?'

'Bee. Is it yours?'

I looked where he was pointing. A bee was working in and out of the heather blossom. 'How on earth should I know who it belongs to?' I said. 'And anyway what does it matter?'

'Matter? I'll say it matters.' He tapped my arm. 'That bee is *thin*.'

He didn't look potty but neither did Crippen. 'My husband's thin,' I said and immediately wished I hadn't. If he was a maniac it would be better to invent a burly husband. 'But very strong,' I added.

He laughed. He knew exactly what I was thinking. 'I'm not daft,' he said and the ee-by-gum accent was somehow reassuring. 'I'm a bee man. Have you got a hive?'

'Yes, it's over there behind the bushes.' I pointed to a clump of nettles in the ponies' paddock.

'I'll look at it for you. Where do you keep your hive tools?'

'Look it really isn't necessary, you know. My husband saw to the hive in the autumn.'

The bee man implied that he would be failing in his duty as president of his local beekeeping society if he turned a blind eye to bees in distress. He may not have been daft but he was certainly persistent.

'They're *not* in distress,' I said crossly. 'They're always buzzing in and out of the hive.'

'I expect you've got plenty to do,' he said, as if I hadn't spoken. 'Just give me a hive tool and a smoker and I'll do what has to be done.'

Sod you, I thought, but I knew when I was beaten and went to ask Brian where the bee-gear was.

'In a box behind the kitchen door. Why do you want it?'

'I've got a bee freak. He says our bees are thin – well, one of them anyway. He wants to look at the hive.'

Brian roared with laughter and said next time he wanted to lure a girl into the bushes he would remember the bee approach. 'Mind he doesn't try to pollinate you,' he called as I walked away from the greenhouse.

There were customers walking round the Garden Centre so I quickly handed over the box of beekeeping equipment and returned to my post. When our obsessive visitor had finished rearranging the hive to his satisfaction he came back holding, to my acute embarrassment, a handful of dead bees. 'Lucky for you I came by I'd say,' he said, sprinkling the little corpses at my feet. One or two customers looked at him curiously. 'They're hungry, Missus – the feeder's empty. Now if you've got four pounds of white sugar I'll make up some syrup for them— '

'No,' I said.

' —and a stainless-steel saucepan. Aluminium sometimes gives them diarrhoea.'

By now I was getting heartily sick of him. 'I haven't got four pounds of sugar,' I said. 'They'll just have to eat flowers like other bees.'

For a moment I thought he was going to offer to drive to the village for some sugar. He kept shaking his head and insisting that 'They must have some syrup at once' so to save further embarrassment I promised to make up the sugar solution that very evening. At last he felt able to leave. Without buying anything.

That evening Brian and I went to look at the hive to see what all the fuss had been about. While Brian poured the true-to-my-promise sugar solution into the feeder I kept a respectful distance. I had had an awful experience the previous year when four or five bees had got inside my clothes. This time I was staying out of trouble. 'Are they really thin, Brian?' I called.

'I don't know. If we had any others to compare them with I might be able to tell but these all look the same. Your friend has cleaned up the hive nicely though. You should have asked him to do the kitchen while he was at it – the hive tool would be just the job to scrape the tar off the kitchen walls.'

About three-quarters of our customers, unlike the bee freak, were a pleasure to serve. A couple we called Darling and Darling because that's all we ever heard them call each other epitomised the sort of customer every gardening shop cherishes. Their garden was their main interest and as there were nearly two acres of it they were always on the lookout for something showy or unusual or just plain cheap. They nearly always agreed on what was to be the main purchase of their weekly visit and when they didn't, one or other would come over to us and say 'I've changed our mind', a phrase which I tried to pinch for my own use with no success whatsoever. Darling and Darling had an Irish setter called Rufus, a calm and happy dog who never peed on plants and was the only dog ever permitted near the display beds. 'Other ranks' were kept out by a notice in big black letters saying NO MALE DOGS – a notice that proved that the pen can be mightier than the sword as even the most neurotic dog owners obeyed it.

Toddlers could be a hazard too, especially the ones that had been armed with pull-along wooden toys. They would stagger round the beds in the slipstream of their parents, clutching at the plant supports for their own support. Invariably they would tumble, taking with them raspberry canes on a good day and standard fuchsias on a bad one. It was tempting to put up another notice next to the dog one NO INFANTS ON WOBBLY LEGS but if we did that the logical conclusion would be to ban other undesirables too. Coke-swiggers, know-alls, Germans— no, it was too tempting. Three-quarters of our customers were like Darling and Darling, we reminded ourselves frequently. We would just have to learn to live with the others.

Chapter Four

THE PREVIOUS OWNERS of our place had run it as a cut-flower nursery and much of the equipment they left was no use to us now that we were in a different line of business. Cone-shaped tin vases, packing material and so on cluttered up badly needed space so we put an advert in the local paper and managed to get rid of most of it. But there was one item that nobody wanted: a vast cold-storage unit, standing on concrete blocks right in the middle of a space we wanted for customers' car parking. Brian priced it at £50, then £25, but despite the fact that it was in working order we just couldn't sell it. So we offered it to the scrap-dealer Alf, who said he would come round the following day and dismantle it.

Before he came we thought we would remove the interior fittings and sweep the floor so that Alf could get to the rivets in the metal plating more easily. We carted out some boxes of junk and then noticed three plastic sacks, each half filled with powder, standing under some shelving. Cautiously, for the sacks weren't marked, we dragged them out into the daylight and peered into their depths. One contained white powder, one blue and the third green. A handful of customers browsing around the display beds looked up as Brian called out jokingly: 'Is there an analytical chemist in the house?' and gathered round to join in the guessing game. Speculation ranged from heroin to cyanide and we all agreed it was pretty stupid of someone to leave unlabelled chemicals lying around.

'Of course the last people emigrated,' offered one of the customers, implying that people who emigrate automatically leave trails of cyanide in their wake. Brian, not wishing to be tarred with the same brush as our predecessors, said hastily that he would put the sacks back into the cold store and lock it. The customers went back to their browsing.

Brian then phoned the local health authority and asked for advice on disposing of possibly toxic material. To our surprise they showed concern not only about the powder but about the refrigeration unit itself – some insulation materials can do your lungs mischief – and said they would send us an expert to sort things out.

The expert was a young man whose chances of becoming an old man seemed remote. For instead of using the tools of his trade, test tubes and bunsen burners and things, he used his *tongue*. He tasted the white powder first. Finding himself still alive after a few seconds he repeated the procedure with the other powders. 'Harmless,' he pronounced and turned his attention to the cold store. He borrowed Brian's crowbar and prised off a section of the plate-metal wall. There was a sandwich filling of yellowing candyfloss stuff which he said was fibreglass, then he dashed back to his car and drove away.

'Well really,' I said, 'some scientist. I wonder why he was in such a tearing hurry?' Brian said it was probably to get back to his laboratory to take the antidote to our mysterious powder – 'A sort of chemical April Fool trick, we think the stuff's harmless but he knows it's lethal.'

'They must have a terrifically high turnover in public health inspectors if they all eat the samples, mustn't they?'

'I should say so. Here, help me get these sacks into the wheelbarrow. We may as well put them out for the dustmen now that we know it's safe.'

'Oh, Brian – the poor dustmen. We may know that it isn't paraquat or cyanide but we still don't know what it is.'

But as a week went by and there were no reports in the local paper of sudden insanity among refuse collectors (Dustman Wants to Become Estate Agent) we had to conclude that experts do know what they are doing after all.

Once the cold store had finally disappeared, the potholes in the new parking area were more noticeable than ever and the strange thing about potholes is that they attract swarms of asphalt layers. These gentlemen are, without exception, innumerate: 'I've overestimated my load, lady' or 'I've got half a ton surplus from today's job – let you have it cheap, sir.' Their ideas of cheap were not ours and we refused all offers of part loads until one day a genuine asphalter drove in. 'Can you help me out?' he said urgently. 'I've got a part ton going off in the back, my boss'll kill me. Can I dump it on your drive?'

'I'm sorry,' I said, 'but we can't afford it. You're the third this week trying to sell us asphalt.'

'I don't want anything for it, honest I don't. Like I said, it's going off.'

At that time I didn't know what 'going off' meant and as it was free I said Fine, dump away. The driver backed his lorry on to the car park approach and pulled a lever to release the tail flap. A hillock of glutinous black asphalt slithered on to the ground. 'Oh, lovely,' I said. 'There's plenty to fill the holes, isn't there? Thank you very much.'

'Thank *you* very much, madam. You will tell your husband it's going off, won't you?'

'Yes of course I will and you don't need to sound so apologetic, he'll be as pleased as anything to get it free.' The driver gave me a peculiar look and drove away.

Over lunch some two hours later I said casually to Brian: 'Oh by the way, one of those asphalt people came this morning – you were busy so I didn't disturb you. He's given us a part ton for nothing; he said it was going off but it looked perfectly fresh to me . . .' I tailed off, puzzled by Brian's horrified expression.

'What time did he deliver it?' said Brian in a what-time-are-you-going-to-execute-me tone, not what you'd call cheery.

'About eleven. Why?'

'Two hours ago? You *moron*. By twenty past eleven it would have gone off. Why didn't you come and get me?'

'What is "gone off" anyway?' The penny was beginning to drop. Even we morons are not that dim. I followed him out of the house and down to the new car-parking space. The little asphalt mountain was still where the man had left it, only now it was as hard as iron. It had, in roadmenders' jargon, 'gone off'.

'Couldn't we break it up with pickaxes?' I suggested and my normally peace-loving spouse who was proud of having once marched alongside Canon Collins to Aldermaston said if he had a pickaxe handy he wouldn't waste it on asphalt. Oh well, at least we were still communicating.

Despite having the right sort of name for shifting mountains the mechanics of doing so were beyond me. Brian said when he was less busy, i.e. never, he would hire a pneumatic drill. Meanwhile we left it and very odd it looked obstructing what was supposed to be the entrance to a car park. We shovelled some sand into the potholes but the area still looked uninviting and customers seeing the first car park full would still park on the road verges, which was slightly dangerous on an A road. It was only after I had painted PARKING on the asphalt heap that we could entice drivers into the new space. Once they were in a lot of them couldn't get out again if another car parked behind them and thus trapped they would be forced to walk round the Garden Centre for longer than they had meant to which was very good for trade and is known as an ill wind.

Right through June the weather stayed hot and thundery. The plants loved it, springing back to attention every time the showers stopped and growing apace in the hot spells. The first sweetpea crop was under glass, their fragile blooms unaffected by the weather outside. They were not the best sweetpeas Brian had grown – standing in a sterile medium chemically-fed once a week doesn't give the exhibition flowers that you get with deep trenching in farmyard manure – but at 10p a bunch it didn't matter. Each morning we would pick a couple of bucketsful and stand them in the lay-by fronting the Garden Centre. Few people could resist anything so gorgeous for only 10p and it was a good lure. They smelt heavenly, especially first thing in the morning when opening the greenhouse doors would release a wave of fragrance reminiscent of our old flowershop.

As the strawberry season came in we added punnets of locally grown strawberries to our trestle table in the road. We only made a few pence profit on these as they were intended, like the sweetpeas, for bait but the experiment was not a success. We found that whole punnets of strawberries were being scoffed by children whose parents were wandering round the Garden Centre and as neither Brian nor I could be strawberry-guarding and serving at the same time we had to bring the trays of strawberries back to the safety of the shop counter. Then we thought we would try free-range eggs at 40p a dozen as an eye-catcher but this had the drawback of attracting people who only wanted eggs and not plants. All in all, the roadside table was more trouble than we had thought. Particularly after the incident of the blackboard.

We kept a blackboard propped up against the trestle tables and each day would chalk up a list of what we considered 'best buys' on that particular day. As well as the strawberries and sweetpeas already mentioned there might be a batch of calceolareas outgrowing their pots and rather than have the trouble and expense of re-potting them we would offer them at a reduced price to get rid of them. Or a few early lettuces grown for ourselves might all heart up together and have to be cut and sold before they bolted. What we wrote on the board was just a straightforward list so when one day every customer drove in laughing like mad we thought they were just happy because it wasn't raining. It wasn't until half-way through the morning that the real cause came to light. One of the customers, a man with a family of small children, said: 'Farting's free in our house.' I didn't say anything because I thought I must have misheard him. 'You'd better wash it off,' he went on. 'It might upset some of the old pussies round here.'

'Wash what off?'

'Your blackboard. Must have been kids.' He rounded up his own tribe and departed. Mystified, I walked down the drive and was stopped in my tracks by the all too horribly clear writing on the blackboard. Under our own list was appended:

Snots	5p
Big Jobs	5p
Farts	10p
Beltchiss	5p
Wees	5p

and underneath that in a still childish but more mature hand:

Maureen Riley	32p

Charging back to the shop to get a wet cloth, I collided with Brian who had been serving some of the 'old pussies' who were our bread and butter. 'Come with me,' I whispered helping him to load their boot with escallonias. 'Some kids have been chalking things on our blackboard.'

Brian was amused by the list, especially the price of Maureen Riley. He said the young lady had probably demanded all the loose change in her young client's shorts pocket. After that we didn't leave any chalk lying around and one budding signwriter was reduced to writing CONSERVATION AREA? in the dust on the back of our minivan. We liked this one a lot and left it there for two years, occasionally freshening it up with a wetted finger.

Serving the customers and looking after the plants kept us busy right through into summer. Stock had to be replenished weekly so as not to leave too many gaps between the shrubs. As for the shrubs, we found we could make do with fewer of these once they had produced their summer foliage because they took up more space but even so there were several dozen of over a hundred species to feed, weed and water. As the trays of bedding plants sold out we moved tender plants – fuchsias, geraniums, begonias – and a few unusual things like schizanthus out of their nursery beds and into public view. They were a spectacular success, particularly the 'non-stop' begonias which threw up cluster after cluster of huge blooms and sold like hot cakes. We stood them on benches in a 120-foot polytunnel and the display was so stunning I didn't really like selling any. My favourites were the deep apricot ones and I often tried to hide them at the back so that we could keep them for a bit longer. I believe some antique dealers suffer similar pangs about parting from their favourite pieces. We priced the non-stops at 80p which gave us a profit of 35p per plant and was still miles cheaper than any we had seen on sale locally. We couldn't always undercut our competitors though. Being small we were unable to bulk-buy certain things. Peat, for instance, was retailing at a near-by

Cash and Carry cheaper than we could get it wholesale and it was the same with Growbags.

On the benches opposite the tuberous begonias we laid out some rows of fibrous begonias, then a thirty-foot block of fuchsias, about twelve varieties. These we priced at 25p. They were nice healthy plants but a bit on the small side and we thought 25p was a fair price. To our surprise they didn't sell at all well so Brian upped the price to 45p and soon there was hardly a fuchsia in sight. It is always a mystery to us why this trick of the trade works but it nearly always does. The ones that were left didn't grow very quickly. They were prone to Anorexia Handbagsia, a disease peculiar to Garden Centres and public parks. The disease is spread by middle-aged women who nip off the growing tips of easily struck speci-mens and stuff them into their capacious handbags when nobody is looking.

The bounty hunters didn't confine their activities to fuch-sias. Pinks and Busy Lizzies were popular targets and even on one occasion a hybrid tea rose. We have never been very successful with rose cuttings so it was doubly galling to be robbed by someone who was apparently a better gardener. We were both too cowardly ever to confront our suspects openly but would sometimes try the mildly sarcastic approach: 'Would you like a bag of compost for your cuttings?' This would invariably produce a bland stare or a self-deprecating: 'No thank you, I'm hopeless at cuttings,' and a firmer grip on the handbag.

One morning we had a real thief and had to call the police. I had gone out and Brian was minding the shop. At about noon which was always a quietish time for business, two men parked their car in the road, walked into the Garden Centre and asked Brian for a couple of pounds of tomatoes. He went into the greenhouse to pick them and when he came out the men had gone and so had our takings for the morning.

I got back to find a panda car parked outside and a policeman chatting to Brian in the shop.

'We've been robbed,' Brian said, pointing to the empty cash box. The policeman looked quite bemused and kept

47

saying 'an *ice-cream* carton' as if he had never seen an ice-cream carton before.

'With a snap-top lid,' said Brian.

'Oh, I was forgetting the snap-top lid,' said the policeman heavily. 'Makes a difference a snap-top lid does. And how much was in this impregnable container?'

'I'm afraid I don't know,' said Brian. 'I've had about twenty customers this morning, all average spenders. I should guess about sixty or seventy pounds and most of that would be one-pound notes.'

'Gordon Bennett,' said the policeman. 'No cheques? Gift vouchers?' Brian shook his head. He was able to give a description of the men but not of their car which had been parked out of sight. The policeman said the best he could do would be to warn other Garden Centres to watch out. There was no chance whatsoever, he said, of getting the money back. 'But I'll tell you what I'll do,' he added. 'I'll start you off again. How much are your double petunias?'

'Ten pence each,' said Brian.

'Is that all? I'll have three dozen, please, mixed colours.' He handed Brian a fiver and we all burst out laughing as we realised that there was no change in the cash box.

'Come indoors,' I said. 'There's plenty of change in the other box.' Too late I saw Brian making horrible faces at me. We filed in to the kitchen where the main cash box stood on a shelf next to the dogs' bowls. There was an embarrassed silence.

'A *shoe box*,' said our new friend in a voice quite wobbly with emotion. 'Labelled "cash". I don't believe it.'

'It's our main cash box,' I explained. 'We tip each day's takings into it and once a week we bank it. There's about five hundred pounds in it.'

The policeman lifted the lid and looked inside. 'By some miracle there is,' he said. 'It must be this elastic band that foiled them.' He took off his hat and sat down before lecturing us gently but persuasively on the need for more stringent safety precautions than elastic bands and snap-top lids.

He was right of course. Times were changing fast and even

small rural shops were at risk now. It was a depressing thought. In all our years of running shops in London the only theft we ever had was when one of the porters at Covent Garden pinched a quarter of toffees out of Brian's van. He was arrested later, not for pinching the sweets but for being one of the Great Train Robbers.

The policeman pocketed his change and put his hat on. 'I'll be off now then,' he said. 'I'm sorry about your incident but it could have been worse, couldn't it? By the way be extra careful on July 5th, won't you? It's the Wimbledon finals.'

We couldn't see what the Wimbledon finals had to do with crime but it seemed that popular sporting events on TV kept so many people indoors that shop thieves could ply their trade with less risk of being caught. We had noticed that on Cup Final and Grand National days there were hardly any customers; it was evidently a case of one man's meat . . .

'Hang on,' I said. 'If we don't do any trade because of Wimbledon there won't be any money for them to steal, will there?'

'Yes there will, there'll be twice as much,' said the policeman. 'Everyone does their shopping in the morning for Wimbledon so you'll have a whole day's takings by lunch time.' He didn't seem to find it at all funny that burglars might actually do their forward planning with the aid of a sports fixtures list and I had to stifle my giggles until he had gone.

Still, we did alter our security arrangements and lectured all three dogs on their uselessness. They were leading rather bored lives now that we were too busy to take them for many walks and they just lolled around in the garden most of the time. They did get some walks but only when it was raining hard enough to keep the customers away. Then Brian (who likes walking in the rain) would put on his waterproofs and boots, triggering off wild excitement among the dogs. After a few circuits round the kitchen off they would all go, leaving me to catch up on badly neglected housework.

During one of their wet-day absences I was just wondering whether to leave the carpets unhoovered for the third week running, tackle the ironing or ignore both and cook something interesting for a change when there was a knock on the kitchen door. Outside stood the most enormous man I have ever seen, not just tall but huge in all directions. He was immaculately dressed in a pin-striped suit and white shirt and was holding aloft, a long way aloft on account of his height, a big umbrella.

'Good afternoon,' he said, bowing ever so slightly. 'Van Eppin,' and he handed me a card which was large and expensive.

'Very nice,' I said approvingly. I am a pushover for good-quality stationery. 'If you'll hang on a jiff I'll put my wellies on and come out. I wasn't expecting any customers in this weather.'

'Your company wrote to my company. I am selling.' He indicated his card. 'May I speak with your director, please?'

'Oh, you're a salesman, why didn't you say so in the first place? You'd better come in for a minute.' While he was getting himself and his umbrella through the door I read his card. He was Dutch and represented a famous firm of bulb growers. From the look of him I would have guessed he owned rather than sold for his company. 'I'm afraid you've had rather a wasted journey,' I said. 'My husband's out and I don't know anything about ordering bulbs. Would you like a cup of tea?'

'Thank you yes. Your husband will be back?'

'Well yes, eventually. He's taken the dogs for a walk. I should think he'll be a couple of hours at least.'

'Two hours? In such weather?' He paused and then said ponderously: 'I am thinking he will be very very wet.'

And very very cross, mate, I thought if he finds you filling up the kitchen when he gets back all ready for a hot bath. I made some tea and cleared a space at the kitchen table. Even sitting down the Dutchman seemed to be standing up. His shirt was so piercingly white it made Brian's unironed T-shirts on the table look like a before and after advert for Persil.

'You should have made an appointment,' I said putting tea and biscuits in front of him.

'I apologise, Madam,' he said. I liked him for that, he

wasn't pushy like most of the salesmen who called. Also he chose the plain biscuits and left the chocolate ones. He wasn't exactly a bundle of fun though, it was like having a robot to tea. I tried to start the ball rolling: 'My son once spent his holidays washing up at Amsterdam airport. He enjoyed Amsterdam – I expect you know it well?'

'Very well.' Long silence.

'Have you got any children?'

'I am a bachelor, Madam.'

Gosh, he was heavy going. The time crawled by. He had only been there about half an hour but it seemed longer. He produced his bulb catalogue but as I was only the 'director's' wife and not the great man himself I didn't even get a sales talk. It was a beautiful catalogue with full-page colour photographs of tulips, daffodils, narcissus and iris. 'Can we keep this?' I asked, thinking how nice it would look if I cut the photographs out and mounted them on the walls of the shop.

'No,' said Van Whatsit. 'This is my copy. I will leave an abbreviated catalogue for your husband. From this he will make his selection.'

'You're going then?' I put his cup and plate in the sink before he could change his mind. He stood up and gave his strange little bow again. 'I am appreciating your hospitality. Now I go to Turkey.'

By no stretch of the imagination could I see that elegant suit in an Istanbul bazaar but then he said something about 'Plymouth after Turkey' and I realised he meant Torquay.

Brian, who was very wet when he got home, was considerably cheered not to be confronted by a sixteen-stone bulb seller. He disappeared into the bathroom and read the abbreviated catalogue while he soaked in Radox. Much too expensive was his opinion, so my boring half hour had been a complete waste of time. Brian's walk however had been productive. He had, he informed me proudly, made an appointment for Noah to go to the hairdresser's.

'Noah? To a human hairdresser?' Since neither of us went to hairdresser's (my newly acquired dog-clipping skills had come in useful) it seemed a bit ostentatious to send a pony.

'There's got to be a catch,' I said. 'What have you been up to?'

'I haven't been up to anything – too damn wet. I met a hairdresser on the moor, she had a collie like Ella so we—'

'Yes, OK. Skip the doggy bits. How did you come to be talking about Noah?'

'Well, this girl – Molly – has got a couple of horses too. As she's a hairdresser I thought it was a good opportunity to pick her brains about Noah's mane and tail.'

'What did you say about his mane and tail?' I said. Noah's hair had been causing me some concern lately. Unaccountable patches had appeared; not the baldness associated with lice or sweet itch but just simply no hair. 'Did you say it definitely wasn't lice or sweet itch?' (Untreated, both these conditions point to an uncaring owner.)

'Mm, I did. And I told her about Magnus perching on the ponies but she said magpies wouldn't pull hairs out unless it was the nesting season. She said you can take him along to the shop where she works and she and her colleagues will have a look at him.'

The next day, during a slack period in our own shop, I saddled Noah and rode the three miles to the hairdresser's. It was on the main road in a small town but there was plenty of pavement space for him to stand safely out of the way of the traffic. I dismounted, led him to the front of the shop and tapped on the plate-glass window. A junior who was shampooing a customer gave a huge grin of welcome and called to the three other assistants who immediately abandoned their clients in mid-treatment and came out on to the pavement.

'Hi, I'm Molly,' said one. 'You must be Noah and Brian's wife.'

'Hullo,' I said. 'It's awfully kind of you to offer to look at Noah. Shall I come back when you're less busy?'

'No, that's OK. Our ladies are all regulars, they won't mind Noah queue-jumping. Isn't he a darling?' The girls fussed and patted Noah, then the junior appeared with a handful of jelly-babies. 'A present from Mrs Dunstan,' she said. 'I've stuck her under a towel to wait. She says she's in no hurry.'

Noah by now thought he was in heaven. Four friendly girls all telling him what a lovely boy he was *and* jelly-babies. He is a greedy pony who puts on weight easily and sweets are very much on the forbidden list.

Molly and her cronies got down to business. They frowned over the state of his mane and tail and one of them produced a pair of scissors. 'I'll do his split ends first.'

'Would you like to use Noah's own comb?' I said.

'No, I prefer mine thanks.' I don't know what the girls' other clients thought of this; they were all peering through the window and must have noticed.

After a lot more snipping and combing, Noah's tresses looked quite presentable. The girls had layered his mane and thinned his tail so that now the unsightly patches merged neatly into the overall shape.

'That's wonderful,' I said. 'How can I keep it looking like that?'

'I'll give you some conditioner for his split ends.'

'And have you any idea what caused the bald patches?'

'Yes, I think so,' said Molly. 'You've got another pony, haven't you, a youngster?'

'Yes, Rory. He's three.'

'Well, I'd guess that young Rory has been chewing Noah's hair. Try separating them for a few weeks.'

Try separating Siamese twins, I reflected as I rode home after a protracted farewell. (Noah had not been at all keen to leave a place where they gave you jelly-babies.)

Predictably, Brian had a mild fit when I told him the plan. 'Divide their paddock? And have them shouting to each other for weeks on end?'

'Neighing,' I said.

'Well, I'm naying too. Try putting pepper on Noah to put Rory off.'

I experimented with a range of substances I thought might deter Rory without actually poisoning him. Eucalyptus, surgical spirit, peppermint and vinegar all acted as excellent fly repellents but not as pony repellents. The solution had to be separation but rather than divide the paddock we decided to kill two birds with one stone and send Rory away to be broken in. Hopefully when he came home he might have forgotten his childish ways.

Local enquiries led me to a girl in her twenties who was fast gaining a reputation as a trainer. So many people stressed how kind and gentle she was that I had no hesitation in sending Rory to her yard. On his second day there I phoned her to see how he was settling in. Fine it seemed; Rory had chummed up with a fellow pupil, a stallion who had had to be castrated late in life and who was suffering post-op blues. 'Rory's cheered him up a lot,' the girl said. 'He's very friendly, isn't he?' I agreed. Rory's little weakness was not mentioned. In any case if he started investigating the rear end of a recent castrate he was liable to get a kick on the nose which would be more effective than eucalyptus.

Back at home Noah was noisily and incessantly demanding to know where Rory had gone. 'I think he'd better have a holiday,' I said. 'He needs company.'

'A *holiday*? What the hell does he need a holiday for? He never does any work.'

'All right then, *not* a holiday – more a change of scene.'

'Perhaps he'd like a cruise? And why not a flight on Concorde for Magnus while we're at it?'

'There's no need to be sarcastic,' I said. 'It's only three pounds a week for communal grazing round here. It would rest our own paddock and give Noah the chance to be with other ponies.'

'Is it really only three pounds?' said Brian, suddenly interested. I could see he was thinking Why don't we make this a permanent holiday?

While the ponies were away there was a spell of glorious weather which meant we were able to make real progress with the outside work. Setting up the Garden Centre had been only part of the overall plan and now that the business was quietly ticking over we had time to see to the five acres as a whole. Hedges had to be cut back, walls mended, paths excavated and the whole property made to look as trim as possible. We reckoned it would take us two years and we were now half-way through the first. If the house itself had not been in such a deplorable state we might have been able to do it in one but there was no point in trying to cut corners with our only capital asset.

The short heatwave saw a dramatic drop in turnover. All Garden Centres expect peaks and troughs during the year, the busiest time being spring. Summer brings the 'just looking' brigade, then there is another upsurge in the autumn when people want a bit more colour in their beds. But this heatwave also brought a most unexpected phenomenon and one which we could have done without. It started with a mysterious disappearance, not of money, not of fuchsias, but of *words*.

Chapter Five

'HAVE YOU ANY Corylopsis Spicata?' asked a woman with a battered Land Rover. Battered Land Rovers usually meant serious spenders so I put on my most helpful face and led her to the hardy shrub section, sub-section Hamamelidaceae, further sub-section spring flowering witch-hazel for ordinary mortals.

'I think we've got two sorts,' I said. 'Big and, er, not so big.' Unless customers specifically asked for miniature things it was best to avoid the word small.

'Glabrescens Gotoana and Spicata?' asked the woman.

'I can't remember,' I confessed. 'I write so many labels the names just become a sort of porridge in my memory.' I picked up the nearest plant and removed the plastic identification tag. It was blank. 'That's odd,' I said. 'I could have sworn . . .' I tried the next one. That was blank too. With mounting unease I walked along the display bed. All the shrubs from Ceanothus to Clematis had blank labels.

'It's impossible. I *know* I labelled them,' I said to my customer. 'I spent hours doing them.'

'Perhaps they washed off in the rain,' she said. 'Oh no, it hasn't rained for a week, has it? And you would have noticed before now if the ink ran.' She stepped across one of the beds and examined the labels on that side.

'They're all nice and clear over here,' she said, 'and here's the very Corylopsis that I wanted. Spicata— oh, *and* you've got Willmottiae. How splendid! I can't resist Willmottiae, can you? – *such* a scent.'

My brain was now running in parallel grooves, one half storing away the fact that Willmottiae was scented (useful ammunition for future dithery customers) and the other half trying to work out what the hell had gone wrong with the labels. I pushed the label problem aside and gave Mrs Land Rover my full attention. People like her were invaluable in that they could, with a bit of a prod, give me a free tutorial as they made their purchases. We had the incomparable Hilliers manual and other less comprehensive but better illustrated reference books but there was nothing to beat personal advice from experts.

She bought both the plants then strolled round the rest of the beds planning out loud what she would buy in the autumn for what position in her acid-based garden. I squirrelled away as much information as I could then as soon as she had gone I fetched Brian to see if he could solve the mystery of the invisible ink.

'It is impossible,' he agreed as we surveyed row after row of blank plastic tags. 'You *did* write on them all. I saw you. And the pens are guaranteed indelible.'

Months ago we had tested the pens thoroughly, writing out some sample labels then trying to wash the ink off. They had remained clear and unsmudged through applications of hot and cold water, detergent and even bleach.

'Got it,' said Brian suddenly. 'They're not lightproof.'

'What do you mean?'

'Well look. It's only the lettering on the *south*-facing stuff that's gone.'

We walked up and down the long oblong beds inspecting the stock from Abelia to Zauschneria. The labels on the outside south-facing plants were blank; the ones on the opposite side were still faintly discernible while in the middle of the beds, where the foliage was thickest, all the words were as good as new.

We were both very angry, I more so partly because I have a shorter fuse to start with and partly because the tedious job of relabelling would be mine. I stormed indoors and dashed off a furious letter to the manufacturers of the pens. Indelible, I informed them, according to the OED means 'that which cannot be blotted out' so how *dare* they market an indelible ink which vanished after a few days in the sun? I demanded an apology and compensation and felt a lot better after I had posted it.

Then came the tricky problem of what to use on the labels now. We had already experimented with all sorts of markers and had only chosen the current pens because they were guaranteed foolproof. Some lead pencils gave good results but it was difficult to stop the point skidding off the narrow labels; also they were inclined to break if you pressed too hard. Freezer pens were easy to use but it would be illogical to suppose that they would withstand light; wax we had tried (lovely clear letters but irresistibly tasty to slugs), and about six kinds of 'gardeners' pens all much too smudgy to be reliable.

'I'll go into town and see if anything new has come on the market since we last looked,' Brian said.

'I'll go if you like,' I said, trying to sound casual.

'No you jolly well won't. It takes a block and tackle to get you out of a stationery shop once you're in. See you later.' And he was gone.

By the time he returned I had made an inventory of the stock to be relabelled, an infuriating exercise running into four figures. Some of the conifers posed a problem in that it was hard to tell what they were. Originally we had laid out conifer species according to habit – spreading, prostrate, etc. – but we had not allowed for the habits of our customers who frequently picked up a plant at point A and abandoned it at point B. To the untrained eye a lot of infant conifers look the same. Our eyes were untrained. I often wonder what the purchasers of our Cupressus Pygmaea must have thought when they found the things shooting up to roof level.

On the whole though, thanks to Hillier-who-should-be-canonised, I think we got the relabelling right. Brian bought some fibre-tip pens which were guaranteed lightproof in three languages. They were good but a fraction too coarse for me to be able to get all the information on a four-inch strip. (The plant labels are longer than this but you have to leave a blank bit to push into the earth.) So I shortened some of the less important words. Camellias became Cam., azaleas Az. and so on. Then came the varieties like Chamaecyparis Obtusa Sanderi (did these wretched breeders never spare a thought for retailers?) – then their nasty habits – Erectus, Pendulus or

Prostratus, then their colours. Many plants have flowers of differing colours but I got so fed up with this second time around labelling performance that I left out secondary colours. This led to more trouble in the long run. Customers would come up to us and say: 'I always thought Cistus Verguinii was white with maroon basal patches. It says here' – peering at the label – 'white. Is it a new variety?' And since neither of us knew everything, and since one of us was inclined to come out in maroon patches herself if the customers became technical, this sort of thing did nothing for our reputation.

Eventually – it took three part-days – I finished the two thousand six hundred and nine labels, and, feeling curiously calm, I phoned the manufacturers of the invisible ink. The firm had trained its switchboard girl to be as obstructive as possible. She didn't seem to know what a managing director was and put me through to someone called Roger. Roger listened to my complaint – he hadn't received my letter – and said I would have to realise that theirs was a young company. I said I hoped it would suffer an early cot death and what was he going to do to compensate us?

'There's no question of compensation,' he said. 'In normal use the pens you allege you used—'

'*Allege*?' I howled.

'—are indelible. The ink has undergone stringent tests.'

'Did you stand it in hot sunshine for a week?' I could hear myself getting fishwifey.

'Prolonged exposure to ultraviolet light does not, in my opinion, constitute normal use. Why don't you get your staff an embossing machine?'

'Our staff,' I said coldly, 'hasn't got time to write, er—' I thumbed feverishly through a book by the telephone, 'Lasiocarpa Arizonica Compacta. Several hundred times.'

'I say, have you got Compacta? The one with the blue leaves?'

'Yes,' I lied. 'Only it isn't labelled. Someone's rotten ink vanished in the sun.'

Roger stopped being human and reverted to type. I threatened him with the Trading Standards Office and Esther

Rantzen but he was unimpressed. Or so I thought at the time. But a couple of days later we received a parcel of six dozen pens with a compliment slip. They had typed the slip which to me was a clear indication that *they* didn't think much of their product either.

During July when customers were thin on the ground (none on the afternoon of the Wimbledon finals) Brian took time off to visit growers and buy fresh stock. It was much better than ordering by phone and saved money in delivery charges. By the start of the school holidays he had been to Worcester, Dorset, Somerset and Gloucestershire, each trip resulting in a sort of botanical musical chairs on the display beds. Unpopular lines like Garrya Elliptica (what a dull shrub that is) were moved to the draughtiest darkest corner to make way for showier plants which we hoped would catch the eye of holidaymakers. We had been told by an experienced nurseryman that holidaymakers are usually on the lookout for plants that stow away tidily in a car boot and for things that would make suitable gifts for cat-minding neighbours. Brian gave a great deal of thought to these neighbours and bought a range of compact and colourful plants for people to choose from.

Sure enough, on the second Saturday of the school holidays, our first homeward-bound holidaymakers drove in. 'Got any plastic windmills?' they asked. Brian's face froze. They went away without buying anything. Later the same day he was asked for a wishing well and I had two enquiries for gnomes. I made the mistake of telling the first enquirer that we had shot the resident gnomes with an air gun. She was genuinely shocked, as if I had said we shot kittens, and hurried away looking quite upset.

But happily it was still only about a quarter of our customers who were dotty. The other three quarters, the Darling and Darling types, were very nice indeed. And there were one or two people like the Jumping Lady and the Geranium Man who didn't fit into either category.

The Jumping Lady seemed ordinary enough. She came in at

tea time one day when Brian and I were having a breather on the lawn outside the house. 'Just looking,' she called. 'Don't get up.' So we stayed where we were. A little while later Brian glanced up from his book and nudged me. 'What on *earth* is that woman doing?' he whispered.

I rolled on to my stomach and propped my book up in front of me so as not to appear nosey. 'She's measuring the holly bushes,' I said. 'Perhaps she's got a gap in her hedge and she wants something that fits.'

The woman who was about sixty put her tape measure away then, to our astonishment, took a few paces back, ran at the line of hollies and jumped over them.

'I think I've got sunstroke,' Brian said. 'I could have sworn I saw one of our customers jumping over the shrubs.'

'She did – oh look, she's doing it again. Hey, Brian, she'll break them. One of them has fallen over. Hadn't you better stop her?'

The Jumping Lady picked up the fallen shrub and put it back in the bed. Then she called out: 'Thank you very much' got into her car and drove away.

'Don't mention it, Madam,' said Brian. 'Bring your friends.'

Half an hour later when we were doing the watering she came back again, this time in a different car. 'You must have thought I was mad driving off like that,' she said gaily. 'I forgot my cheque book *and* I came in the wrong car. This one's more suitable, isn't it?'

'Yes,' I said cautiously. More suitable for what?

'I want two or three dozen bushes,' said the Jumping Lady. 'All the same height if possible.' Brian, who was moving the sprinklers, nearly jumped over the beds himself when he heard her. A sale of two or three dozen would put a very agreeable strain on the shoe box. 'So I brought my daughter's car,' the J.L. went on. 'The boot's much bigger than mine'

Our euphoria was short-lived. She didn't want to buy the shrubs but to hire them. Her daughter was organising a Pony Club rally and wanted some strong bushes to use for jumps. She had tested, i.e. jumped over, the hollies and would like to take twenty-four 'And a dozen of those Christmas tree things, please. They look good and strong.'

'I'm not sure what to charge you for hiring,' Brian said. 'We've never been asked before. What about breakages?'

The J.L. knew all about hiring. 'I do it every year,' she said. 'I leave you a cheque for the full amount and you give it back to me when I bring the bushes back. I don't think any will get broken but if they do I'll pay for them. You can charge me a fiver if you like for the actual hiring.'

We stuffed twenty-four Ilex and twelve Picea Abies into her daughter's car and prayed that every one of them would get broken so that we could keep the cheque. But hollies and Christmas trees are so horribly robust that they all survived the Pony Club rally intact. Still, the fiver was better than nothing.

There was nothing dotty about the Geranium Man. He was the producer in a London film crew which was on location in Devon to make a TV commercial. 'Morning luv – governor in?' It was refreshing to hear broad Cockney again.

'No, he's just gone out,' I said. 'Will I do?' He said I would do very nicely and how about eight o'clock tonight. After a bit more banter in this vein he explained the real reason for his visit. The film crew needed daffodils for their day's shooting programme.

'*Daffodils*? In August?' Patiently I explained the life cycle of spring bulbs.

'It's tricky, isn't it?' he said. 'Trouble is, the product's yellow and Derek's got the script all set up for daffodils.'

'What is the product?' I asked, but he wouldn't say. He walked over to his van which was full of equipment and cameramen and told them about daffodils. 'That sodding Derek,' a voice cried petulantly. 'This is the second time. Remember the snow in June?'

The producer turned to me. 'Where's your old man gone then?'

I was annoyed at the implication that Brian would be able to conjure up daffodils. 'He's gone to the osteopath,' I said. 'He hurt his back humping peat and he has to go twice a week.' The producer seemed to find this amusing and relayed the joke to his cronies inside the van. After a short conference they decided to alter the absent Derek's shooting script and go ahead with daffodil substitutes. Four men got out of the van and surveyed the beds of summer flowering plants.

'They're nice,' said one, pointing to the massed geraniums. 'Got them in yellow?'

I counted up to ten then showed them calceolareas, salpi-glossis, mimulus and begonias. They took out tape measures and I thought here we go again. Why were we cursed with customers who measured and jumped? Why couldn't they just buy?

'We'll take the geraniums in the nine-inch pots,' said the producer at last. 'Sixty should be enough.'

I have a forgiving nature. Sixty at £1.80 each, that was um . . .—

'Won't be a jiff,' I said. 'I left my handkerchief indoors,' and I sprinted back to the house for my ready reckoner.

Brian's mother, Addy, was staying with us at the time. She was busy at the sink when I rushed in and looked round in surprise. 'What's the hurry?'

'Sixty geraniums at one eighty?'

'Really? How lovely. Brian'll be pleased.'

'I need a *total*. Have you seen my ready reckoner?'

Addy sighed: 'It's a hundred and eight pounds, stupid. Who's the customer – a village fête?'

'A film crew. They're making a TV commercial.'

'Well, you tell them to make something nice for a change. Something like the puppy and the Kleenex.'

I went back to the shop and made out a properly receipted bill for the producer's expense account. He gave me a cheque then backed his van up to the geranium bed. The men started to load the geraniums and it was soon apparent that arithmetic was rearing its ugly head again. Sixty into one wouldn't go.

'Have a heart, Trev,' complained a six footer. 'We'll never get in on top of that lot.'

'Perhaps Derek was right about the daffodils,' said the producer. 'We could have stacked them up on their sides.' He scratched his head then came up with a brainwave. 'We'll hire them,' he beamed. 'We don't want to cart that lot all the way back to London. We'll bring them all back here tonight, eh luv?'

'Oh, all right,' I said sulkily. 'But you'll have to pay for any damaged ones.'

'Course we will. Right boys, in you get – it's only for a few miles. Lennie, Tom, get in the front with me and you two fit yourselves in the back. Mind how you go with them flowers.'

I'll never forget the sight of those hulking great men crammed into a small van with sixty geraniums. All except the driver cradled an armful of pots, their faces completely obscured by flowers.

'Thanks a lot, see you later,' called Trev and drove carefully out.

Brian came home shortly afterwards and said he was sorry to have missed the fun.

'You'll meet them tonight,' I said. 'You can work out how much to charge them for the broken stuff.'

'Oh well, it'll be nice to have a conversation in my native tongue again.'

But the meeting between the 'governor' and the geranium man didn't take place after all. Towards the end of the day when Brian and I were both seeing to customers we heard Addy calling: 'Brian – can you help me up – I've had a fall.'

'Where are you?' Brian shouted.

'In between the greenhouses.' Leaving our customers to serve themselves we ran across the lawn and found Addy sprawled across a metal cold frame. 'I was doing some watering,' she gasped. 'I tripped over the frame. Ooh, my leg hurts.'

'Is it your bad leg, Mum?' said Brian anxiously as we helped her up. She had had a kneecap removed and was supposed to be careful with that leg.

'No it's not my knee, thank goodness. I've cut my shin.' Holding on to our arms for support she hobbled slowly back to the house.

'Don't fuss,' she said as I started to prepare a bowl of water and Dettol. 'Go back and see to the customers. I'll be all right in a minute.'

Brian made her a strong cup of tea while I cut her stocking

off and washed some of the earth from her shin. The cut was appallingly deep and the skin had been torn right off the tibia. She laughed ruefully: 'That's put paid to my chances for the Olympics.'

'Goodness, you're brave,' I said. 'How can you *laugh*? If this was my leg I'd be yelling for morphine.'

'I've seen a lot worse in the blitz,' said Addy briskly. 'Hurry up with that tea, Brian. Florence Nightingale here seems to be letting a lot out.'

'Sorry,' I said, 'but it's best to let it bleed cleanly for a while to fetch out the dirt.'

'Here you are, Mum, I've put plenty of sugar in,' said Brian. 'I'll get a field dressing while you're drinking it. You've gone a bit white.'

'Of course I've gone white, Brian, I haven't got much blood left up this end. And I don't want any of your field stuff on the cut either.' She sipped her tea and I emptied the basin of blood down the sink. Brian fetched some sterile dressings from the bathroom and applied a huge gauze pad over the cut. He has done a first-aid course and is very deft with bandages.

'I thought you meant lime or nitrogen when you said field dressing,' said Addy, but now shock was starting and her voice quavered a little.

Brian phoned the local cottage hospital on the off-chance that they might have changed their policy since we were last there and keep a stitcher on the premises. As luck would have it, their visiting doctor was still doing his ward rounds and would be free to stitch the leg immediately. Like most octogenarians Addy was not keen on hospitals and went very quiet as we helped her into the car and tucked a blanket round her. Her leg must have been throbbing like hell but she didn't complain.

Just as Brian was driving out Trev, the geranium man, drove in. The two vehicles inched past each other and Brian called out: 'Sorry – can't stop. Got to get to hospital.'

Trev stared at him open-mouthed. 'What *again*?' he said. 'Hardly worth coming home, was it?'

The film crew, still garlanded with red blossom, unfolded

themselves from the van. Whether it was reaction after Addy's accident or what I don't know but I found I simply couldn't stop laughing. 'Very nice,' commented Trev sarcastically. 'Your old man's down the 'ospital again and all you can do is laugh.'

'It's not him this time,' I tried to explain. 'It's his mother – she . . . she . . .' and I dissolved into helpless giggles.

'The old lady's down the 'ospital? Blimey, I never knew it was such a dangerous business running a garden centre. Watch out for them geraniums, boys, they'll have your throats.'

Trev's flippancy was very much on the surface. Once I had pulled myself together and told him the story he couldn't have been nicer and was as concerned about Addy as if she had been his own mother. He and his crew unloaded the geraniums, most of which were looking haggard after their show business debut. 'They need a drink,' I said, more to myself than anyone in particular, but Trev asked one of the men to turn the sprinklers on and see to the plants.

'No, it's all right, I'll do it later,' I said. 'Now, what about the broken ones? I don't really know what to charge you.'

'They've *all* been knocked about a bit,' said Trev firmly. 'Give me the cheque back and I'll give you fifty quid cash.'

This turned out to be a very good deal as within a week or so the geraniums had recovered enough to go back on sale. Brian repriced them at £1.20 having first trimmed off their broken shoots. Fittingly these shoots, now cuttings, provided occupational therapy for Addy while her own damaged limb was mending. She had had fifteen stitches in the leg but could still manage to sit at the kitchen table to pot cuttings during the last few days of her visit.

It was soon after this incident that seasonal fall off in trade gave us the opportunity to take a break from work. We were both getting bored with being on duty seven days a week and needed a change of scene, so Brian overhauled our fishing tackle, brought two day licences for a local reservoir and shut the shop. GONE FISHING I chalked on the door and off we went for a whole day. The sun shone and there was lovely silence, punctuated only by the click and whirr of well-oiled reels and the occasional Mole-like remark as we studied the water.

Eight hours later midges discovered the delights of human flesh and we had to go home. The perfect day was further enhanced by finding messages weighted down with bricks outside the shop from our cryptic clue brigade. They seemed to have had quite a little shopping spree in our absence but by then it was too dark to go searching under flowerpots for their money. We took the notes indoors and worked them out over supper.

'Roses are red, violets are blue, two pounds thirty if you solve this clue.' Brian shook his head.

'Go on. What's the rest?'

'That's all. Pass the bread, please.'

'Here's one in green ink. I bet it's that Isadora Duncan.'

'Oh no,' Brian groaned. Isadora Duncan was a chiffon-swathed woman who had once offered him her body in payment for plants but as it wasn't much of a body he had held out for cash.

'She'll get you in the end,' I said, passing him the note.

'Not until she puts on a few stone, she won't. Do you think "roses are red" actually means roses? It's a bit obvious, isn't it?'

'Mm. Anyway we haven't got any roses for £2.30. Try mixing red and blue.'

'Ah yes. Something purple for £2.30. That narrows it down.'

'We could do with a metal detector,' I said. 'I'm sure other shopkeepers don't have to go digging for coins in sand beds.'

'We've let them get into bad habits,' Brian agreed. 'We should have trained our regulars better right from the start. And perhaps we shouldn't have told them about the robbery – they're burying the money in more and more difficult places.'

It *may* have been pure coincidence but we found we had done a better day's trade on our day off than we did when we were both on the premises ... Perhaps burying money satisfies some basic human need? Either way, it certainly gave a new meaning to the word turnover.

Another 'time off' venture for me was dog clipping. It wasn't as restful as fishing but it gave me a break from the work at home and the chance to meet dog lovers rather than garden lovers. I had done very little clipping since my training course, just friends' dogs and my mother's mongrel, Inky. Poor Inky. Basically she is a poodle cross but because I needed practice in different breeds she had in the past eight months found herself fashioned into all manner of shapes – Schnauzer, Airedale and even Bearded Collie. As my mother said, by the time I had finished with Inky she was not so much a poodle cross as a cross poodle.

After I had decided that the time was right for me to take on a few dog customers I put the word out on the bush telegraph. This sort of advertising is cheaper than newspapers and, I hoped, would limit replies to a manageable number.

'Are you the dog lady?' said my first enquirer. I nearly dropped the phone with excitement – my very first paying dog!

'Yes,' I said, pencil poised over diary. (Never answer your phone without your notebook and pencil. Dear Alison – my Cockney tutor's voice sounded in my inner ear.)

'I want you for Ron,' the voice continued. 'I'm seventy-two and my husband's got a rupture. We used to be able to manage but Ron seems to know we can't control him. He's a devil, a real devil.'

I swallowed nervously. 'Could I have your name and address, please?'

She launched into an endless story about Ron and how sweet he used to be when he was a puppy. 'He's still good-natured,' she said doubtfully, 'but of course he doesn't get the exercise he needs now that my husband's got this rupture. You'd better bring a muzzle.'

I wrote muzzle. I had never used one but there's a first time for everything. I asked Ron's owner for her name and address again and Ron's age. ('Don't take geriatrics if you can help it.' Further words of Alison's wisdom rose from my memory. 'Sometimes they drop dead under the blowers.') Ron's owner gave me directions to her home and we rang off.

I waved the diary triumphantly: 'Brian, look – I've got a booking for tomorrow. It's a three-year-old called Ron.'

'Marvellous. What an extraordinary name.'

'It is, isn't it? Specially for a – oh *no*.'

'What?'

'I forgot to ask what breed he is.'

Chapter Six

'NOT A VERY professional start,' Brian observed.

'How could I be so *stupid*?' I said.

'You've had a lot of practice. What sort of dog did he sound like?'

'Oh, he had a middle-European accent,' I said coldly. 'What a bloody silly question.'

'You know what I mean. Did the owner refer to him in any way? She might have said "Ron needs a new basket now that he's four foot six" or something like that.'

'She said he was a devil, a real devil and I was to bring a muzzle.'

'There you are then. He's big. He's ferocious. Shall I phone the hospital this time or will you?'

'*Shut up*. I'm nervous enough already. It's a pity they're not on the phone or I could call back and find out what he is.'

I spent the evening poring over my dog manuals and checking my equipment. Honey gave me a look of dismay when she saw the case of gear and hid behind the settee. Ella and Parsley who were not so quick on the uptake each had to act as Ron's understudy as I fumbled with the intricacies of a leather muzzle.

'You won't let *my* customers see you leave tomorrow, will you?' Brian grinned. 'Or anybody else? Choke chain, muzzle, leather gauntlets – it's hard enough to get rid of some of the travelling salesmen as it is. How much are you going to charge for this, er, service?'

'I don't really know,' I said. 'It depends on the condition of the dog really. If he's been well cared for I can get straight on with the clipping but if not I may have to spend ages untangling the coat. I imagine he'll be a medium-sized terrier so that'll be about four pounds if he's in good condition and about five pounds if he isn't.'

'You're a rotten liar, you know. You don't imagine he's a medium-sized terrier at all.'

'True,' I admitted. I had been trying to blot out the memory of Rex Harrison's savage fangs. And that had been in the security of a well-ordered training establishment. 'All right then – ten pounds for Ron the Ripper.'

Finding a BEWARE OF THE DOG notice on Ron's garden gate the following morning did nothing for my confidence. A gravel path led to a neat cottage. There were no teeth marks on the woodwork and I felt better.

'Good morning, dear. Come in, come in.' Ron's owner Mrs Johns, a cottage-loaf-shaped old lady, welcomed me in. 'I shut Ron in the kitchen,' she said. 'I daren't let him come to the front door, once he gets out we'd never catch him. Now, are you ready? I'll open the kitchen door.'

She walked along the passage and I stayed where I was, nice and near the exit. Suddenly a white tornado hurtled out of the kitchen and rushed at me with excited yelps. Ron's impetus carried him along the carpeted floor so fast he couldn't stop and he ran up my jeans. I clamped my arms round him and started to laugh.

'I'm so sorry, dear. I told you what a devil he is.'

'I was expecting a bigger devil actually. He's a Lhasa Apso, isn't he?'

'Yes that's right. That's clever of you. Most people think he's a Shih Tzu.'

'Most people think he's a bloody lunatic.' This was the voice of the ruptured husband resting in the sitting room.

'Dad's grumpy today,' said the old lady. Ron struggled in my arms. 'I think you've got him the wrong way up, dear,' she said absently. I put him down and he leapt round and round on what were presumably his back legs. Lhasa Apsos look more or less the same at either end.

'Isn't he sweet,' I said, following Mrs Johns into the kitchen.

'He is when he's asleep. He's on the go all day long – makes

71

us tired just watching him. Now where do you want him first, on the table or in the sink?'

'On the table. I'll catch him – oops, missed. Perhaps if you stand there you could grab him on the next circuit.' It took the two of us five minutes to corner the energetic little creature. He fizzed with life and thoroughly enjoyed teasing us.

At last I had him on the table, struggling like a fish. 'Watch his teeth,' warned Mrs Johns. 'He's wild when he gets over-excited. Did you bring a muzzle?'

'Not one that would fit him. Isn't he tiny under all that fur?'

'Good things, small packages. Isn't that right, Ron Ron?'

Lhasas are not normally clipped, their long flowing coats being their chief attraction, but Mrs J was not bothered about Ron's looks. She wanted him tidy and manageable. 'I've got arthritis in my hands,' she said. 'I can't comb him properly and as for bathing him, well, I wouldn't like to attempt it. Could you give him a short back and sides, please, so that it doesn't trail in the dirt, and make a hole in his face for him to see through?' She left me with these somewhat unorthodox instructions and went away to get on with her own work.

I pinned Ron down with one hand and parted his forelock with the other. He had dark intelligent eyes and looked at me with an expression of sheer insolence. 'Well, young sir,' I said, 'one of us has got to be the boss and I'm very sorry to tell you it's going to be me.'

Ron had other ideas and tried to leap off the table. Alison would have said 'shorten your chains' but Mrs Johns' kitchen was not equipped with overhead hooks and chains. I slipped a choke chain round his neck and gave an experimental tug à la Barbara Woodhouse. Ron was furious and showed his tiny teeth; I could quite see why his owner called him a devil.

'Stop it,' I said sternly, and shook the choker again. This time Ron took careful aim and latched on to my finger. His teeth were not very sharp and for all his bravado there was no real malice in him.

'Oh well, if that's how you're going to play, Ron, you've asked for it. You can have your bath first.'

72

The effect of water on mutinous dogs is truly astonishing. On the training course I had seen wildly resisting dogs calmed down as if by magic once they were under the tap and now the same treatment worked on Ron. I connected my rubber hose to the mixer taps and soaked his coat from head to tail with lukewarm water. Within seconds all the fight went out of him and he stood in the sink shivering with fright while I shampooed and rinsed, shampooed and rinsed, and applied conditioner. Mrs Johns came in to get a dustpan and brush and chuckled when she saw her bumptious Ron. 'Dad, come and look at this,' she called. 'Ron's shrunk in the wash.' Dad appeared, brown-eyed and white-haired, not unlike Ron.

'Well I never,' he said. 'What's happened to you, Sunshine?'

They went away and I wrapped Ron in a towel and carried him back to the table. He was so subdued it made me feel rather mean and when he forgivingly licked my hand it was too much to bear. 'Have a choc drop,' I said, 'and for goodness sake let's be friends.' He thumped his tail on the table and wolfed a handful of choc drops. But the water torture must have been uppermost in his mind for he was now a very different Ron, quiet and so co-operative I was able to blow-dry his coat and comb out the tangles with no bother at all.

Mrs Johns made me a cup of coffee at half-time and we let Ron get off the table to stretch his legs. 'You've worked a miracle,' she said. 'He's not jumping up and down any more.'

'It wasn't me, it was the water,' I said and told her about the training course and some of the useful tips I had picked up.

'You could try bathing him yourself,' I suggested, realising even as I spoke that this was no way to build up a regular clientele. 'Once I've trimmed his coat short I don't think you would have any trouble bathing him and as you can see he's as good as gold after a soak.'

When he had had his haircut Ron no longer looked like a Lhasa Apso but he did look tidy and comfortable. I am not keen on leaving fringes hanging over dogs' eyes; it must be so irritating for them not to be able to see where they're going, so with Mrs Johns' approval I fashioned Ron into a sort of Cairn terrier shape.

'There you are, Ronald, all finished.' I lifted him down.

'That's a lovely job,' said Mrs Johns. 'Go and show your dad, Ron.' Ron trotted off to the sitting room. 'Dad'll be pleased,' she said. 'He's always wanted him to look more masculine and it'll be much easier to keep him clean. By the way his name's not Ronald it's Oberon.'

'Oh,' I said non-committally.

'Awful, isn't it? Oberon Truly Fair of somewhere or other, that's his Kennel Club name. My husband said he wouldn't be seen dead walking round the village with an Oberon Truly Fair so we called him Ron.'

A mobile dog clipping service unearths some odd characters but not often one as odd as my next customer, Miss Edmonds. She rescued abandoned cats and dogs and gave them the run of her large house with ten acres of jungly grounds. She hardly ever went out unless to collect another stray to add to her collection and ordered food and things by phone. I don't suppose I would ever have met her if Brian, in conversation with a Garden Centre customer, hadn't mentioned that his wife clipped dogs. The customer, who happened to be a neighbour of Miss Edmonds, told him that Miss E had about a million dogs.

'A million dogs,' Brian reported later. 'If you could get a regular contract from the owner of a million dogs we could retire.'

'You could, you mean. I'd be wearing my fingers to the bone.'

'No – you'd sub-contract the work. Go on, phone her. I've looked up the number for you.'

'Oh, all right. But she's bound to have her own equipment if she really has got so many dogs.'

There was nothing to lose so I dialled the number: 'Miss Edmonds? My name's Faith Addis. I've recently started a mobile dog grooming service in this area and I wondered—'

'Are you married?' The question took me completely by surprise.

'Married? Well, yes.' Good God, I thought, what next – my blood group?

'Would you be coming on your own? To do the dogs?'

'Definitely. My husband's a nurseryman. The dog side of things is my department. Someone told us that you had, er, some dogs. Quite a few I understand.'

'Fourteen. Neutered.'

'Oh, how sensible. It stops them peeing on the shrubs, doesn't it? The males anyway. I find bitches— '

'Mrs Addis, there are far too many unwanted creatures in the world. I see to it that mine do not add to the number. How much do you charge?'

'Three pounds an hour for well-behaved dogs and extra if I get bitten, ha ha.'

'Mine are well behaved.'

'I'm sure they are,' I said ingratiatingly. 'Have you any who need clipping at the moment?'

'Yes I have. You've phoned at a most convenient time. Hendrix and Motley are too hot in this weather – they're both long-coated mongrels – and I think they would both be more comfortable if they were clipped out completely. I used to have my own clippers but they wore out and new ones are so expensive.'

'A hundred and twenty one pounds plus VAT,' I said.

'Good heavens. I think I paid about five pounds in— well, quite a long time ago I suppose. Can you come at ten o'clock tomorrow? And you will be on your own, won't you?'

Brian was quite hurt when I told him about Miss Edmonds. 'What on earth has she heard about me?' he complained.

'Nothing. I told her you were a nurseryman.'

'Did you? Sounds good, doesn't it? She sounds sinister though.'

'No, she's not sinister. I think she's so wrapped up in her dogs she doesn't want more than one visitor at a time.'

I was wrong again. Miss Edmonds didn't mind how many *female* visitors came to see her and her animals but she wouldn't allow any men. She had not had a man over her threshold in thirty years she told me. She hadn't had a floor cloth over it either, I noticed, when she let me in. Heavens, what a filthy house. 'What an unusual house,' I heard myself say.

'Do you like it? I cut down all the laurels in the shrubbery – horrid gloomy things. I like to see sunny rooms. Ah, Hendrix dear, this is Faith. She's going to clip that heavy coat for you. And Motley's.'

'Hullo Hendrix,' I said, kneeling down to stroke him. He was a beautiful dog, slightly bigger than a retriever, with a thick black coat. He licked my face then sauntered out of the room. Several other dogs and cats jumped off chairs and window ledges and came over to say hullo. There was a tranquil air about the place rather like a monastery and although all the surfaces were covered in muddy paw marks it didn't smell at all doggy.

'Which one is Motley?' I asked.

'Motley is probably in the garden. Hendrix will tell him you're here.'

I looked at her to see if this was some sort of leg pull but she wasn't smiling. She showed me where to plug in my electric clippers – in the *sitting* room of all places. 'I'm afraid I'm going to make rather a mess in here,' I said. 'Wouldn't you rather I worked in an outhouse or the kitchen?'

She gave a ghost of a smile and said No, the dogs were used to being groomed in their sitting room. So I spread out a large sheet I carried for the purpose and unpacked my case. It was a pity, I thought, that she didn't want me to use the kitchen; I was dying to see more of this unconventional house.

'Would you like to go to the lavatory before you begin, Mrs Addis?'

That was odd. Had she read my mind? And why was I Mrs Addis to her but Faith to the dogs?

'Call me Faith, if you like,' I said, 'and no thanks, I'll go later.'

'Very well. I'd better go and get Hendrix if you're ready.' She went to the door and called along the hall: 'Hendrix, don't be all day, Faith is waiting.'

Hendrix reappeared and Miss Edmonds showed him where he was to stand on my sheet for all the world as though he was a person being measured for a suit. This mode of address was catching. Instead of saying 'sit' or 'stand' to Hendrix which is how I normally talk to dogs I found myself saying: 'Would you like to sit for a moment while the clippers cool down?' and then: 'Right, up again please, Hendrix.'

I could see Miss Edmonds approved; she sat in one of the armchairs enveloped in cats and watched me work. Once she said: 'You've got a good face', which I thought was a nice thing to say until on reflection I wondered if she meant I looked like an Alsatian.

An 'all over' clip is just about the easiest cut to do on a dog. I carried a range of cutter-heads from very fine to very coarse and Miss Edmonds chose a Number 7, a medium blade which leaves the coat short but not shaved. Hendrix's fur was thick but in such good condition it fell smoothly under the whirring clippers. Motley trotted in as I was doing the last leg and stopped short when he saw the pile of fur. He was pretty, a brown and white fluffy mongrel with one ear up and one down.

'Come in, Motley, you fool,' said Miss E gently. 'I told you Faith was coming this morning so you needn't look so surprised.' But Motley had vanished. Miss Edmonds shook some cats off her lap and stood up. 'I'll have a word with him.'

I brushed Hendrix and let him have a good shake before he got off the sheet. Then I rolled it up, complete with fur, and spread out a clean one for Motley. 'Is he nervous?' I asked Miss E when she came back carrying Motley. She considered the question for a while and then very quietly and unemotionally told me how Motley had been found lying by the side of a motorway after someone had thrown him out of a car. 'Basically he's not a nervous dog,' she said, 'but obviously after such an experience . . .'

'And Hendrix,' I said, 'was he a motorway case too?'

'No. Hendrix was found tied up in an outhouse with very little food. He had been there for six months.'

'Oh, I'm sorry,' I said.

'It's all right. You didn't know. I'd have people like that publicly flogged. Would you like a cup of coffee?'

'Not at the moment thanks. I'll do Motley first, then have coffee if that would be all right.'

Miss Edmonds wanted a longer cut for the fine-coated dog. I changed the blades over, switched the motor on and let it run for a moment to get Motley used to the noise. He glanced at Miss Edmonds for reassurance. She ignored him and settled back in her cat chair, the picture of relaxation. Motley put two and two together – if she's not bothered by this machine I don't need to be – and stood like a trained show dog while I clipped him. Wisps of his gossamer-fine hair floated all over the room but Miss Edmonds said it didn't matter, she would sweep it up some time.

After the job was done she invited me into the kitchen for coffee and here I had another surprise – the kitchen was clean. Not insanely clean, the way some people like kitchens, but normal with modern units and a vinyl-tiled floor. It was such a contrast to the rest of the unwashed house it caught me unprepared. Miss Edmonds smiled almost apologetically and said: 'I don't think the dogs approve of vinyl floors but one must insist on hygiene in the kitchen, mustn't one?'

I couldn't make her out at all. Yet another facet of her intriguing personality was her taste in television programmes. There was a big colour set in the kitchen and over coffee I asked her jokingly if the animals liked TV. She said they slept through everything but that she herself was addicted to boxing, wrestling, football and 'The Sweeney'. I couldn't see how this fitted in with her complete ban on men in the flesh as it were and it's not the sort of thing you can ask someone on first acquaintance.

At about this time, on one of my non-clipping days Brian asked me to man the shop as he wanted to clean out the well. Strictly speaking he didn't want to but fronds of aquatic flora were starting to appear in the domestic cold-water supply so he had to. He chose a day when our water-sharing neighbours were away, ran the taps until the well was low, then looked down the hole. 'Whew – come and look at this.'

I leaned over the well. The dogs and Small, who always like to know what we're up to, leaned over the well too and I wished I had had a camera handy to capture their faces peering goggle-eyed into the black depths. Mysterious plops could be heared down below, plops which I thought might be frogs. 'You will be careful not to kill any frogs, won't you, Brian? I'll get you a clean bucket to put them in if you like.'

Brian, who was not looking forward to being cold and wet, said something extremely rude about frogs and I thought I had better go away and leave him to scrape in peace. Frondy stuff, a white spaghetti-like plant, had attached itself to cracks in the brickwork and spread out like a science-fiction growth. Brian proposed scraping it off with a trowel first then scrubbing the walls of the well with a wire brush. He lowered a ladder down, stripped to his shorts and climbed in holding a bucket and trowel over his arm. Ella, who had been getting more and more agitated as she watched the proceedings, sat back on her haunches and began to howl.

'Stop that blasted row.' Brian's voice was distorted by the well.

'I'll take the dogs indoors. Ella's worried about you,' I called. 'She probably thinks you're burying herself.'

'She's not far wrong, it's *freezing* down here. Will you bring me a hot drink in about an hour? And take that noisy animal away.'

I shut the dogs in the kitchen and, to be on the safe side, Small too. Brian had enough on his plate without having to play pussy's-down-the-well with Small.

Customers trickled in and I was kept busy for the rest of the morning except for one lull when I made Brian a mug of Ovaltine. He was blue with cold and in a fairly bad mood after wrestling with sodden water weeds. 'Can't stop,' I said hastily. 'I'll leave your drink on the edge here and get back to the shop.'

One of the customers was a woman who had recently bought a holiday cottage and wanted colourful climbers for a dull wall. She was accompanied by her two children, a boy and a girl aged about six and seven, who soon grew bored looking at plants and wandered away. 'Don't go near the road,' their mother called.

'I'll get them some toys,' I said. 'Then they can play on the lawn and you can browse as long as you want to.' And spend lots and lots of money. I gave the children a box of toys but they said they would play with the big dog. 'Your Lassie,' said the boy. 'We played with him when we came in the Easter holidays, don't you remember?'

'No, I didn't know you'd been here before.' They looked crestfallen so I added hastily, 'I must have been out. I'll get Ella for you – she's a her by the way not a him.'

Ella and Parsley bounded on to the grass and I left them to amuse the children while I went back to their mother. Unhampered by anxiety she was completely engrossed in choosing plants and as I had other customers to serve I left her to her own devices. After about twenty minutes the children rushed up to her.

'Mummy, guess what? We've found a *human head*.'

Their mother, deliberating between a Virginia creeper and a Russian vine, murmured automatically: 'Don't put it on the car seats.'

'Mummy, you're not listening. A real human head. Ella led us to it.'

'It spoke, Mummy. It said what the hell are you doing here?'

'Is that the way you go to hell, Mummy? Down a hole in the ground?' They dashed off.

I burst out laughing at the bemused expression on their mother's face and explained about Brian cleaning out the well. She called after the children: 'It's not a human head, it's Mr Addis', and I wondered whether to rescue Brian from his young audience or to stay at my post and make money. Business sense won.

'The Russian vine is quicker but the Virginia creeper is more colourful,' I said.

'I think I'll have both. *And* these clematis. Do you think they would suit a west-facing wall?'

Meanwhile Brian had given up the unequal struggle to clean

the well with the children leaning precariously over the rim and had climbed out. I tried to ignore the shrill cries of excitement and Ella's frantic barking but my customer thought she had better not presume on my husband's good nature (?) any longer and called the children back. They returned with arms full of spaghetti weed. 'I'm going to play cooking with mine,' said the little girl.

'You're not,' said the mother with absolute certainty. 'You're going to throw that smelly stuff away and get in the car.'

'Oh *Mummy*.'

'Hey, Mummy, the man had Ovaltine— well, he would have had, only I knocked it down the hole. Can we have Ovaltine? We haven't had Ovaltine for— '

'*Paul*,' snapped his mother. 'In the car. Now.'

Grumbling, the children climbed into the car. 'I think that man had a tummy-ache, don't you, Paul? He had a tummy-ache sort of face on, didn't he? Mummy, can we have a dog like Ella?'

'Don't ask her for a dog now, silly. We won't get Ovaltine if we ask for a dog.'

Their mother and I exchanged a 'who'd be a parent' look. 'You could always slip some brandy into their Ovaltine,' I suggested. 'Put them out for a couple of hours.'

She laughed, gave me a cheque for the plants, and drove away. I envied her going home to a clean dry husband who had probably been playing golf all morning. 'I bet he won't have a tummy-ache face on,' I said to Parsley.

Brian dripped into the kitchen and huddled over the Rayburn. His back was coated with green algae and he smelt like something the dogs had dug up.

'Hullo Dante,' I said, 'what was it like down there?'

'Wrong chap,' he grunted. 'Dante's place was hotter. Listen, I've been thinking— '

'I'll run you a bath,' I interrupted, knowing from long experience that any thinking on Brian's part meant trouble.

'We're not stretched enough here,' he went on.

'Not *stretched*?' I squawked. 'Good God, Brian, it must have been cold down that well. You're hallucinating. Arctic explorers do it if their body temperature drops too low. I'll get you a bigger towel.'

'I don't want a bigger towel. I want a bigger project than this piddly little place. I think we should move.'

'We *are* going to move. As soon as we've got the place ship-shape. Five acres and a grotty house is stretching me, I can tell you, and at the end of it we should get twice what we paid for it.'

'But if we had a *bigger* place,' he argued, 'a much *much* bigger place and we did it up we could make real money, not just a few thousand. We're good at houses, in fact I'm beginning to think it's the only thing we are good at, so why don't we look for a place we can really get our teeth into?'

There seemed no point in reminding him that we had been so busy stretching ourselves in the Garden Centre, no work at all had been done on the house. Tar still streaked the kitchen walls, mushrooms grew on the bedroom ceilings and the conservatory still looked like a brothel. 'Go and have your bath,' I said. 'I'll make you some soup.'

I could quite see how being forced to spend a morning stuck down a clammy brick shaft and then being deprived of one's Ovaltine could unhinge a person. But surely a hot bath followed by hot soup would put a stop to all this Thinking.

But it didn't and that's why, a week later, I found myself changing trains at Wolverhampton en route for North Wales.

Chapter Seven

FIVE YEARS PREVIOUSLY, during the same year that Brian and I had come to Devon to seek our fortune, some friends of ours – Rob and Ellie – had also left London and set up a smallholding, theirs being in North Wales. Each couple had followed the other's progress closely; each had made the same mistake of starting out without enough capital and each had run up a huge overdraft. For years Rob and Brian had been in favour of the four of us pooling our resources (can you pool overdrafts?) and going in for a big project together. But apart from the fact that Rob and Ellie didn't want to live in Devon and we didn't want to live in Wales no big project had so far suggested itself. Latterly Rob and Ellie had moved into a caravan while they renovated their farmhouse for resale, a situation not unlike our own purchase of a derelict nursery for renovation and resale.

Now, it seemed, a property had come on the market which would not only fulfil Brian's wish to be stretched but might solve both families' financial problems. It was a hotel on the north coast of Wales going for a song because it had fallen into disrepair. The beauty of the idea, batted between Rob and Brian by letters and phone calls, was that a brewery was prepared to lend the whole of the purchase price at a low interest rate in return for a contract from the new hotel proprietors.

Brian spent hours figuring things out on paper. Rob had sent him all the details – the hotel's turnover, wages bill, rates and so forth – and Brian agreed with Rob's assessment that if we could get the hotel spruced up and running efficiently its market value would be in the region of a quarter of a million pounds.

'Could you bear Wales for a year or two?' Brian asked.

'I could bear a wigwam in the jungle for a share of a quarter of a million,' I said. 'Oh no, maybe not the jungle, too many spiders.'

Brian had explored North Wales before we left London and had found the inhabitants hostile and the villages bleak. It had been the time when several English-owned holiday homes had been victims of arson, an activity which had inspired the slogan: Come Home to a Real Fire – Buy a Cottage in Wales. I had been to Snowdonia twice but had been put off it, not so much by the natives as by Brian's relatives. They used to take walking holidays there every Easter. Directly after breakfast up they would go to the top, bounding like springboks, and as I have not the build nor the inclination to struggle up mountains without a pony I had not enjoyed the expeditions.

'This would be strictly business, wouldn't it, Brian?' I said, suddenly remembering Snowdon. 'You wouldn't expect me to do anything hearty, would you?'

'Do you mean walking? I doubt there would be much time for whole days off. Anyway you've got Noah.'

'And Rory,' I reminded him. I was impatient for Rory's return. Brian's mind was on hotels and he didn't want to talk horse. 'We must both go and see it,' he said, 'and meet the hotel staff. They may not like the idea of English people taking over.'

I suppressed a vision of Welsh Nationalists shinning up the hotel drainpipes to murder us in our beds. 'Can we go together?' I said hopefully.

'Not really. There wouldn't be time to drive there and back in a day and we can't leave the Garden Centre unattended overnight. I think you should go up by train and stay with Rob and Ellie to see how you like the area. Don't look so apprehensive, you've got Welsh ancestors so you'll be all right.'

'I don't think extremists ask to see your pedigree before they knife you. Anyway my lot came from Pembrokeshire. Nice and friendly they are in Pembrokeshire *and* they all speak English.'

'Well, I'm sorry,' said Brian in exasperation. 'I'll ask Rob to move the hotel to Pembrokeshire. You can always wear a leek in your buttonhole for protection.'

'That's garlic and devils. I'll take my sheepskin coat though. And winter boots.'

'Good grief, you are optimistic, aren't you? If the Nationalists don't get you the weather will, eh?' He went to the desk and fished out a railway timetable. I was to change at Wolverhampton, otherwise the journey was straightforward.

So here I was at Wolverhampton, home of the once great Wolverhampton Wanderers. Poor Wolves, they had wandered too far in recent seasons, right down into the second division. I climbed aboard the Wales-bound train and had the misfortune to sit next to a weird man who wanted to talk. No sooner had I opened my book when he peered over my shoulder and said 'Ghosted'.

'What?' I said.

'Books. They're all ghosted.'

'No they're not.'

'Yes they are. Take this.' He tapped his own book, an Alistair Maclean paperback. 'Never wrote a word himself. The printers employ special writers to do it – they write all the bestsellers. Ghosts they're called. What are you reading?'

'John Wain. It's a reissue of one of his early—'

'Not his own work, take it from me. My cousin's a printer – he knows all the dodges. Famous people haven't got time to write books. Did you really think John Wayne wrote that? He's a film star.'

Luckily the train was half empty so when Superbore was distracted by the arrival of a coffee man I took my overnight bag from the rack and fled to the next carriage.

I love train journeys. To sit and read or just look at the view, while someone else argues about whether to turn right or left; what a perfect way to travel. And yet there are people who write and complain if their train is a bit late. I would be more likely to complain if it was early – Dear British Rail, I paid for a six-hour journey and I only got five and a half hours. Please send refund . . .

'ALL CHANGE.' A porter's shout interrupted my musings. The train had stopped at a tiny station and carriage doors were opening.

'Change?' I said to a man on the platform. 'I thought this went all the way?'

'No, you have to finish on the Toytown train, Madam. There's a very steep gradient ahead.'

Everybody got off and crossed to the other side of the platform where a small train was waiting. It was more like a tram than a train with wooden seats, lino floors and no heating. The doors slammed and we were off again, through breathtakingly beautiful mountain scenery. Some local women laden with shopping had boarded the little train and talked loudly among themselves in Welsh. They were all dressed warmly in winter coats and I giggled to myself remembering what the weather had been like when I left Devon – hot enough for shorts and T-shirts. Snowdonia was cold, August or no August, and I was glad of my own warm coat.

Rob met me off the Toytown train. Formerly bearded he was now cleanshaven. 'A sacrifice,' he explained, 'to make a good impression while I was shopping around for bank loans.'

'I expect you miss it, don't you, in this climate?'

He laughed and said Brian and I had gone soft in equatorial Devon. 'It's bracing here,' he said. 'And what about the scenery? Isn't it wonderful?'

I agreed wholeheartedly. With Rob you could admire a mountain safely and not run the risk of being conducted up it. 'I don't suppose you even possess a pair of walking boots, do you, Rob?' I said. 'Brian's got two pairs, his old ones wore out but he keeps them for muddy work.'

'Wore out? Phew, what a terrible thought!' We drove for about half an hour with the windows closed and the heater turned up full and caught up on family news.

'So Brian wants to be stretched, does he?' said Rob. 'Ho hum. I don't think you'd find anything more stretchworthy than this.' He swung the car across someone's courtyard and pulled up. '*Voilà*.'

'What do you mean *voilà*? Where's the hotel?'

'In front of you.'

'Which bit of it?' I said, gazing at a façade measuring several hundred yards.

'All of it. I told you it was going for a song.'

'But, Rob, this place is as big as Buckingham Palace.'

'Strictly speaking it's bigger. I don't think Buck House has two hundred bedrooms.'

'And it would all be ours?' I felt faint at the thought of the hoovering.

He nodded. 'Every brick. And the courtyards of course. Are you going to stay in the car looking like a goldfish or shall we get out?'

I turned round to look for the door handle and received another shock. There, not a stone's throw from the hotel, was the sea; masses of it, noisily crashing itself about. Not being overfond of oceans I said accusingly: 'You didn't mention anything about a sea in your letters, Rob.'

'Not mention the sea? Of course I did. I told you the hotel's on the coast.'

'*On* you said. If something is described as on the coast I don't expect to find it half submerged.'

'It is very rough today,' he admitted, 'but it's what the guests come for – Atlantic rollers on the doorstep. It's great for surfing.'

We got out of the car to be met by a wind that was not so much bracing as blasting. Salt spray stung our faces and what with that plus the roaring of the waves, conversation was impossible.

'IRELAND'S ON THE LEFT,' Rob yelled. 'AMERICA STRAIGHT AHEAD.' We struggled across the hotel forecourt and entered through a doorway marked BAR. Groups of men with faces mauve from cold were crowding round the bar ordering drinks. 'They're from the RAF station at Holyhead,' Rob said. 'This is their watering hole.'

'Poor things,' I said. 'They look frozen. Why doesn't someone put the heating on for them?'

'Because,' said Rob with a grin, 'if they're cold they'll buy spirits. Anyway, nobody puts the heating on in August. Come on, I'll show you part of the ground floor first.'

I was flabbergasted by the size of everything. There were high ceilings ('might have to lower the ceilings to save on heating bills'), rambling kitchens and wine cellars, guest lounges, TV rooms, more small bars – the tour was positively exhausting and I don't think we covered more than half the area. A ballroom, conference hall and squash courts were 'somewhere' Rob said but I wanted to see some of the 200 bedrooms so we skipped those and went upstairs.

Here it was easier to see why the place was going for a song. The roof leaked, quite badly in places, and dozens of the bedrooms were unusable. Many window frames, particularly those facing the corrosive sea spray, had rotted away from the brickwork. Every single one of the bedrooms that I saw needed redecoration and some needed reglazing as well.

There were guests in one wing ('hardy annuals' Rob called them) who said we were welcome to look round their rooms and yes they were having a lovely holiday thank you. Wet swimming costumes, snorkels and flippers adorned the bathrooms, causing so much condensation it was hard to tell the difference between the weather outside and in.

With some difficulty we made our way out of the maze of corridors and found a stairway back to the main bar which was now serving another lorryload of RAF personnel. Rob showed me a photocopy of the hotel's books for the current season; the profit on the alcohol alone was staggering, enough to pay staff wages and leave heaps over for roof repairs. 'And that's without the turnover from the resident guests,' Rob said. He had plenty of ideas for improving the guests' facilities and for building a centre for surfers and skin-divers. Having had his own very successful wholesale business at Covent Garden he knew the importance of pleasing the customer. Like Brian, it was only his need for change that had drawn him into smallholding. 'Would you like a drink while we're here?' he said.

'Good idea. Orange juice, please.'

Rob elbowed his way past the servicemen and returned with two orange juices. We sat on plastic-covered chairs at a plastic-coated table and wondered how much a scrap-man would give us for them.

'He'd probably charge to take them away,' I said. 'And talking of charging, I wonder if those men know how much they're being overcharged for their drinks?'

'They wouldn't care,' Rob said. 'They've got nothing else to spend their money on in camp.'

'But isn't it illegal to make three hundred per cent gross profit on a bottle of whisky?'

'I don't think so. The prices here are the same as any pub's.'

We watched the men down glass after glass and I was surprised to find a puritanical streak in myself that I had never known was there. What a waste of time, what a *senseless* way to behave. Half of them would be legless before the evening was over and have headaches the next morning.

'Do you drink, Rob?'

'Not really. Wine occasionally, or beer if it's hot, but not spirits. Why – do you disapprove?'

'I think I probably do. I haven't worked out why yet. If we came here would we have to serve behind the bar?'

'Not you and Ellie, definitely not. Brian and I might have to though.'

'Brian would hate it.'

'I wouldn't actually like it myself but one or other would have to be around if only to stop the staff getting their fingers in the till.'

I suddenly felt very tired and we decided to call it a day. There was too much to take in on one visit.

Once back at the farm my mind stopped going round in circles. It was so peaceful, the farmhouse and buildings tucked into a valley between mountain ranges; rather cold and windy but blissfully pastoral after the harshness of the sea. Ellie had prepared a roast-pork dinner, quite a feat in the cramped galley of the caravan and with a toddler underfoot.

Their other child, five-year-old Graham, greeted me with: 'Guess what? I've had a sister since you last saw me. She has to go to bed earlier than me because she's two and a bit years younger. Her name's Gwen.'

'I know,' I said, 'and you've got a dog called Gus and a white cat called Humphrey.'

'There Graham, that surprised you, didn't it?' Ellie laughed.

'I've got a magic telescope,' I said. 'It can see for miles and miles.'

'You haven't,' Graham said. 'There's no such thing.'

'A magic telephone then.'

'Ask your magic telephone what I'm going to have for Christmas. Does it do Christmas?'

'No, it can't do the future, only what's already happened.'

'Do you know what happened when our cows got out? Mummy and Daddy shouted at each other. Mummy said Daddy was a— '

'Graham, eat your dinner,' Ellie cut in hurriedly.

'Don't mind me,' I giggled. 'I know how Mummies and Daddies shout at each other when the cows get out. It used to be pigs with us.'

'We had a pig,' said Graham through a mouthful of pork. 'He was nice.'

'I want a pony for Christmas,' piped up Gwen, averting what could have been a dodgy moment if Graham had pursued the pig theme. 'A violet one.'

'It's her new word,' said Graham helpfully. 'I read it to her out of her colouring book.'

'A pony for me and a pony for Graham,' Gwen continued, obviously thinking that since her request for one pony had not been dismissed out of hand she might as well up her bid. But Graham didn't want a pony. He wanted a remote-control lorry with reverse gears. Rob and Ellie made a great show of looking at their watches, a most effective ruse for quietening children at ten minutes to bedtime. 'They want to talk,' Graham whispered to Gwen.

'No we don't,' said Ellie. 'We just want *not* to talk about ponies and remote-control lorries.'

After the children had been put to bed, Ellie made coffee and we chatted about the hotel until our own bedtime. I badly wanted to be as enthusiastic about the venture as they were and yet . . .

Sleeping on the problem didn't solve it and it was not until I was on the last leg of the train journey back to Devon that the issue became clear. Sometimes, when you see a recipe in a magazine you can tell at a glance that it's not for you so you skip it and open a tin of sardines instead. Similarly, the question of whether or not to buy the hotel answered itself once the ingredients – the pros and cons – were set out on paper. There were far more cons than pros.

At the top of the pro list, on the assumption that a trouble shared is a trouble halved, I put 'working with Rob and Ellie'. Then came four or five more factors ending with 'share of x amount of money when we sell it'.

On the con side, number one was 'having the sea on the doorstep', number two was 'being polite to drunken service-men', and the list continued in this vein to factor ten: 'Arctic weather in August.'

Now Brian must go and see the hotel and give his verdict. If he voted 'yes' that would be three to one and I would have to bite on the bullet and become Mrs Trust House Forte for a couple of years.

As the train headed west, we passengers peeled off so many layers that by the time we reached Exeter the carriage looked as though we had been playing strip poker.

'Told you you wouldn't need a coat,' Brian said as I got off.

'Listen, my tropical flower, I have just been to polar regions. Everyone was in winter gear in Wales.'

'I don't think we should go to Wales,' he said.

'I've just been – or didn't you notice that gap in the house? Do you mean you don't want to go and view the hotel? You'll take it on trust?'

'I don't want to take it at all. Rob phoned while you were on the train and told me about the place being practically in the sea. The gardens must be awfully sandy.'

'Gardens? Ground-up rocks actually – that's what it felt like when it blew in your eyes.'

'In that case we've got too much to lose. I've been adding up the pros and cons while I was waiting for the train. Get in the car and I'll show you.'

We got into the car and exchanged lists. Although the wording was different (where he had put 'substantial profit on capital investment' I had put 'lots of money') the lists were

91

virtually identical. Top of his hate items was 'serving behind a bar' and top of his pros was 'partnership with Rob and Ellie'. Both of us had put the money last.

It makes you feel a bit of a twit to discover something fundamental about yourself so late in life. Here was a small fortune being handed to us on a plate and we were turning it down for no better reasons than not having a fertile garden (his), not having a country outlook (hers), having to stay up late and be nice to people (both) and having to wear thermal underwear all the year round (both, but more keenly felt by him as nothing would induce him to).

But turn it down we did and not wishing to go it alone, so did Rob and Ellie. They moved back to England and set up a successful business. Gwen got her two ponies and also two baby brothers for good measure.

Perhaps fortunately there wasn't time to hold a did-we-do-the-right-thing type of post-mortem as suddenly there was an upsurge of trade in the Garden Centre. Holidaymakers without children or dogs and not wanting plastic windmills and gnomes turned up in increasing numbers. There was plenty of good quality summer stock left and this we offered at clearance prices to make room for the follow-on of hardy perennials.

The joy of customers with empty cars is that they are easily persuaded to buy masses of stuff. Half the time I'm sure they didn't know just how much they were buying – Brian discovered he had a talent for packing goods into cars so tightly that the customers would buy some more to fill up the space. One couple arrived in an estate car and went into raptures over our low prices. They bought enough plants to stock Kew Gardens and I thought even Brian wouldn't be able to load it all. When eventually they finished choosing and opened the back of their car it was to reveal two huge multi-coloured parrots sitting untethered on a perch inside.

'Ah, aren't they *gorgeous*,' I enthused. 'Why are they in your car?'

'Well, it's their holiday as much as ours,' said the man matter-of-factly. His wife told us the parrots liked nothing better than long car rides – 'Especially going round corners,' she said. 'They lean like motorcyclists.'

'But don't hotel proprietors mind you turning up with parrots?' I asked.

'Oh, they don't stay in hotels – they'd hate chopping and changing. They're perfectly happy in the car, they've got all their own things with them and as you can see they're not tied up.'

'Don't they ever fly away?'

'Of course they do. Then when they've had enough they come back.'

Brian, who was wondering how on earth he was going to load up this mobile bird house, eyed the parrots warily. 'Don't mind them,' said the woman. 'They'll enjoy having the shrubs in the back with them. I think I'll put the begonias in the front though in case they rip the petals.'

I'll never forget the way Brian kept saying 'Excuse me' to the parrots as he arranged the container-grown shrubs neatly round their perch. They shuffled backwards and forwards examining each plant and giving little squawks of pleasure as their space filled with greenery.

'You stop that,' said the woman as their hooked beaks began tweaking at the foliage. They cocked their heads sideways and looked at her intently while she read them a very mild riot act. I stroked their feathers and she gave me a beautiful red one that had fallen out. Then the crammed car moved off and we saw for ourselves how the parrots balanced themselves by leaning at forty-five degrees when the car turned left and then came upright again when it straightened out.

Although the parrots were the most exotic creatures we ever saw in the Garden Centre other customers often surprised us with the contents of their car boots too. One – Mrs Fish we called her – always had a few buckets of mackerel in hers. The first time she came, she offered to barter mackerel for a half sack of tulip bulbs. It was, as she said, 'friendlier than money' and as we were no strangers to the bartering system we agreed.

'I think you'll find that twenty-three is exactly right,' Mrs Fish said, with such an air of confidence it didn't occur to us to question her equation (personally I would never have the nerve to question someone else's arithmetic anyway) or to wonder what either party would do about change if the price of the bulbs wasn't 'exactly' twenty-three mackerel.

She became a regular customer but we had to ask for cash after the first visit or we would have been living on mackerel for years. Neither of us liked to ask why she always had a boot full of them.

Then there was the dictionary woman. She bought some camellias which had started to show roots through the bottom of their pots. 'They're quite muddy,' I said. 'Shall I lay out some newspapers in your boot for you?'

'No, don't do that,' she said. 'I've got all my Dick and Harrys in the boot. Put the camellias on the back seat.'

'You've got *what* in the boot?'

'Dictionaries. They mustn't get wet.' She lifted the lid of the boot and showed me piles of brand-new dictionaries, all different sorts and sizes.

'Are you a publisher's rep?' I asked.

'No they're mine, mine. They're not for sale.'

'All right,' I said soothingly.

'You've got your own I expect?' she said.

'Yes. Three.'

'Three? I've got dozens. I have to keep replacing the ones that wear out.'

Never having worn out a dictionary I couldn't think of a thing to say, so I loaded her back seat with camellias in silence.

'You're not cross with me, are you?' she said. 'I'm sorry I can't let you have one but I do need them myself.'

'No, I'm not cross,' I said, trying not to sound cross but it was irritating to find oneself unjustly accused of coveting dictionaries. 'But I am curious to know why you cart them around with you.'

Now it was her turn to be cross. She banged the car boot shut and locked it, then she said stiffly: 'How much do I owe you for the camellias?'

'Fifteen pounds thirty, please.'

She counted out the right money and thrust it into my hand. 'There you are,' she said. 'Now you can buy your own.' And with a crashing of gears she drove away.

Chapter Eight

FRAYED TEMPERS WERE not confined to the customers. Brian, in common with most men, always blows a fuse if he finds his razor less than razor-sharp and comes storming out of the bathroom to seek revenge on whoever is responsible for blunting it. Now that both children had left home there was nobody but me in the firing line on these not infrequent occasions.

'What do you mean, you *didn't* shave your legs? There's the proof – hair in the razor. It's bad enough you pinching my last blade but leaving it all clogged up really is adding insult to injury.'

'I meant to clean it,' I said lamely, 'but after I'd done the ponies' legs I thought— '

'*Whose* legs?' Brian's roar sent the dogs scuttling under the kitchen table. 'Did you say ponies? You've been shaving *their* legs with *my* razor?'

'When they came back from their hol— from being away, I found bot eggs on their front legs,' I explained, 'and it's so difficult to pick bot eggs off with your fingers. Of course, I didn't know it was your last blade.'

Brian now really flew off the handle ('It would be more civilised to live with a gorilla than with you' etc). Seeing I was not exactly flavour of the month I took my tea and toast and slunk off to open the shop early hoping that when we next met, at lunch time, he would be less sore. Ella, who simply hates people shouting at each other, elected on this occasion to ally herself with me. (As well as being a pacifist she also stays fairly neutral, siding with whoever is being less noisy.) As things turned out I was glad of her company.

Later in the morning a couple drove in, he dressed in an eye-catching white robe down to his feet and his wife in

96

Mayfair mode complete with a leopard-skin jacket that made me want to refuse to serve them. But shopkeepers can't afford to take a moral stance and I did nothing but send out hate waves in her direction. The husband, brisk and businesslike, handed me a list of plants saying he knew nothing about gardening but wished to purchase two of everything on the list. The plants – over a hundred pounds' worth – were all of the commonplace pyracantha, escallonia type of shrub and we had plenty in stock. 'No problem at all,' I said. 'Do you want them delivered?'

'No, I'll take them with me now. The gardener wants to make a start. There's plenty of room in there.' He indicated his car, an immense hearse-like Bentley. I think I was supposed to gasp with admiration but I must have disappointed him. The only cars I admire are ones that have proved they start first time in cold weather.

'Could you back it up to the shop front, please?' I said.

'No. You bring the plants to the car.'

Rat, I thought, I bet you snap your fingers at waiters too. I fetched a trolley and loaded it with some of the shrubs on his list. Three times I wheeled the packed trolley from the beds to his car. He made no effort to help but leaned against the bonnet drumming his fingers on the radiator emblem.

'Whew, that's the lot.' I put the last plant into the car – the floor space could have accommodated a ballroom dancing display – and handed him back his list. 'That's a hundred and twelve pounds sixty pence, please.' I knew I had totalled it correctly because I'd double-checked while I was loading the last trolleyful.

He walked round to the passenger door and ran his eye over the shrubs. 'I'll give you eighty-five pounds,' he said.

'If you're questioning my total, add it up yourself,' I said touchily. 'All the plants have got price labels.'

'I don't care what the total is, lady. I said I'll give you eighty-five pounds. Cash.'

'You're barmy,' I said. 'Why on earth should I let you have over twenty pounds off?'

'Call it a discount for quantity.'

'I'm not calling it anything. If you can't afford to pay, you shouldn't have ordered so much in the first place.' I was beginning to feel frightened and angry. There was nothing to prevent him getting into the car and driving away without paying. Brian was out of earshot and there were no other customers around to help me.

'I'm waiting,' said the man. 'Are you going to take the eighty-five or not?'

'No. I'm going to unload all the plants and put them back.'

'All right. Call it ninety-five.' He took out his wallet.

Suddenly I had an idea. 'Ella, come here,' I called loudly, trying to convey to her that this was not a game. Ella, dozing in the shop doorway, woke up and shot across the car park towards me.

'Call him off,' said the man in alarm. 'I don't like dogs.'

Although it hadn't been my intention to frighten him with Ella, it was comforting to realise that I could. 'We keep six guard dogs here,' I said. 'Luckily for you this is the quiet one.' And trying to stop myself from giggling I knelt down and whispered to Ella: 'Fetch Brian.'

Ella's brain, which we had always assumed to be a hundred per cent cotton wool, rustily whirred into action. She didn't exactly zing like an arrow to Brian's side but she did fetch him. It's her one and only asset as a dog – if one of us tells her to fetch the other she does. She probably watches old Lassie films in secret.

I don't know who was more relieved to see Brian striding towards us, my haggling customer or me. 'He won't pay his bill,' I said.

'Women don't understand these things,' said the man, plainly thinking everything would be all right now that he had a fellow male to do business with. 'She didn't want to accept eighty-five pounds in cash.'

'His bill is a hundred and twelve pounds sixty and he doesn't like leopards,' I added.

'Dogs I said, lady. I don't like dogs.' He turned to Brian: 'I'm sure you don't like paying income tax, right? What'll you give me for cash?'

To someone whose dearest wish is to earn enough to start paying income tax the offer fell somewhat flat. Brian looked at the car and the fur-clad wife (who had been sitting in the car doing nothing all this time) and then at the plants. He checked the total on my sum. 'This is correct,' he said giving me an incredulous sideways glance, 'but if you can't afford to pay for so much all at once I suggest we unpack your car and start again.'

The man became very agitated and said something to his wife in their native tongue. Brian and I took all the shrubs out of the car, then Brian handed him his list and invited him to pick the ones he intended paying for. He retaliated by withdrawing his offer of cash and getting out his cheque book.

'Sorry chum,' said Brian. 'The cheque card's limit is thirty pounds. And do hurry up, you've wasted a lot of my wife's time already.'

For a moment we thought he was going to drive off in a huff but he changed his mind and wrote out a cheque for thirty pounds. 'Give me thirty pounds' worth of the biggest plants,' he said and went to sit in the driver's seat while we reloaded the back. As soon as we had finished and shut the door he started the engine and departed without a backward glance.

I slumped down on the trolley. 'I don't know whether to laugh or cry,' I said. 'What a creep, what a bastard. And that wife – did you *see* what she was wearing?'

'Dead cats. Is that why you wouldn't give him a discount?'

'He didn't ask for a discount. He waited until I'd loaded all the stuff into the car and then he said he'd *give* me eighty-five pounds for it. Hey, do you think he'll stop the cheque? He's horrible enough, isn't he?'

'He might. Let's cash it before he has time to phone his bank. I'll mind the shop just in case he comes back and you go to town and pay it in. You can ask the bank for special clearance while you wait.'

'OK. I'll go straight away. Is there anything else we need while I'm at the shops?'

'Yes. A packet of razor blades.'

*

A day that had started off with a domestic tiff followed by a row with a customer was bound, by the law of bio-rhythms, to have a third mishap up its sleeve. It came at dusk in the shape of six loose bullocks.

We were indoors looking forward to a visit from friends who were on holiday in Devon when all the dogs started barking. 'Oh good, that must be Reg and Sheila, they're nice and early,' Brian said, and went to open the door. '*Jesus*,' he screeched and grabbed a broom.

This is not the way he normally greets his oldest school-friend. I deduced that Jesus and the broom meant the bell had gone for round three on this most difficult of days. 'Trouble?' I said.

'Bullocks,' he said, rushing outside. My stomach hit the floor. One in a china shop would be bad enough but several in a Garden Centre a calamity. Before joining him, I tied Honey and Parsley to the legs of the kitchen table. Honey was old and Parsley fifty-seven days pregnant; neither would be an asset in a cattle round up.

The bullocks were Herefords, a docile breed which was something to be thankful for. However they were young, playful and horned so I armed myself with a rake and a dustbin lid. Brian was shooing them away from the geranium bed with a broom. 'Stand by the raspberry canes,' he shouted. 'I'll drive them back on to the road.'

Reg and Sheila, arriving a few minutes later, didn't have time to remember an urgent engagement elsewhere. No sooner were they out of their car than they were each issued with a shovel and a confusing set of orders – 'Reg, cut them off before they get to the greenhouse. Sheila, you help Faith. Guard the shrubs. This way, Reg.'

'I'm scared of cows,' Sheila protested.

'They're only youngsters,' I said. 'Just playful.'

'Get that in writing, love,' Reg advised and hoisting his shovel over his shoulder went to help Brian.

'How are you, Sheila?' I said.

'I was fine before we got here. You didn't tell us you were keeping cows again.'

'They're not ours, they must have escaped from someone's

field.' We prodded one of the bullocks away from the sand beds and stood guard until Brian and Reg had gathered all six animals together.

'Let's join up in a line,' Brian said, 'and try driving them in a bunch.' Infuriatingly, the bullocks scattered as we encircled them and one headed straight towards the geraniums. There it braked sharply, its hooves cutting a groove in the sand. 'I'll kill you,' Brian yelled, and hurled his broom javelin-fashion at the animal's rump. Having got the other five together he didn't want to break our line of defence by going after it. Reg seized the nearest missile, which happened to be a horse-shoe, and threw it hard at the bullock's head. His aim was magnificent and from a distance of some forty feet the horseshoe clanged against one of its horns. It drew back in alarm, geraniums trailing out of its mouth, and dashed back to the safety of the herd. 'It's telling the others what an awful headache you get if you eat geraniums,' Reg laughed. 'What's next, Brian?'

Before Brian could regroup us for another attempt at getting rid of the bullocks an agitated farmhand came along the road in a tractor. 'You seen my beasts?' he called. His dog barked insults at Ella who had been supervising the proceedings from a safe distance.

Brian indicated the churned-up lawn and dung-splattered paths. 'There are six here. How many have you lost?'

The farmhand wasn't interested in numbers but in what harm his precious bullocks might have suffered at our hands. He looked them over anxiously. 'You got laurel, Mister,' he said accusingly.

'I didn't ask them for their blasted names,' Brian said. 'Just get them off my lawn, would you?'

'He means laurel – the plant,' I said. 'It's poisonous.'

Brian cheered up visibly. 'Yes, we've got lots of laurel,' he said, '*and* rhododendrons.'

'Shouldn't be allowed,' the man grumbled. ''Tis dangerous to beasts leaving unfenced laurel and rhododendrons where they can get at them.'

Brian, foreseeing a situation where compensation claims would be for damage caused *to* and not *by* the bullocks, briskly reminded the man of the law relating to farm stock. 'Get them off my premises,' he concluded, 'and keep your gates shut in future.'

Still grumbling, this time about holidaymakers who left gates open, the man instructed his dog to remove the bullocks. Ella waited until the party had disappeared into the twilight before emerging from her hiding place and giving one very small defiant growl.

Reg said: 'Can we play another game now? You say "Hullo, Reg and Sheila, how are you?" and we'll say "Hullo, Brian and Faith, good to see you" and then you invite us indoors for a drink and a chat. How about it?'

'Oh Reg, if you only knew the trouble I'd gone to, laying on that cabaret for you,' Brian said reproachfully. Sheila looked at her sandalled feet, green with dung: 'What do you lay on for your enemies, for heaven's sake?'

Parsley gave birth to her fourth and last litter in September. Her previous husband, Nimbus, had pleaded a headache sixty-three days beforehand and a new spouse, Jethro, had been called upon to oblige at very short notice. Jethro was an ex-show dog, 'ex' because one day he had suddenly tired of the limelight and bitten a judge. Apart from this one lapse (which I regarded as showing a degree of intelligence unusual in a pedigree animal) he had good character references and an excellent stud record.

Their union was blessed by three daughters – Pansy, Poppy and Polly – and two sons, Snuff and William. Dear obliging Parsley, seeming to know the difficulties I have with arithmetic, always had litters of five, a dead easy number when you come to work out their feeds in fluid ounces.

Pansy, the first born, showed her father's independent streak from the first. Noisy, restless and energetic, always crawling out of the nest and getting wedged between the bedding and the edge of the basket, she was more trouble to Parsley than the other four put together. Brian too found her little buzz-saw voice trying. He has an ambivalent attitude to newborn pups at the best of times; obviously he's fond of them but he doesn't like it when they monopolise my time to such an extent that their washing – five changes of sheets a day for the first week – means that he never gets a clean shirt. And weighed against the novelty of having a spotlessly clean kitchen he has to put up with the place reeking of Dettol and a wife who never stops quoting bits from Juliet Bairacli Levy's dog book. (Published by Faber, the best fiver's worth a dog owner could buy.)

'When are you going to start advertising them?' he asked pointedly on the tenth day.

'After Christmas. This is her last litter and I want to enjoy them as long as possible. Actually, Pansy could go at nine weeks if anyone wants her.'

Brian said he wished he had gone long ago and where was I proposing to house the little tyrants once they were mobile?

'Oh yes, housing . . . I wanted to talk to you about that. Do you remember me telling you about a woman who house-trained a litter of puppies at six weeks?'

Brian sighed. 'No, but I can guess what's coming. You want to try one of your crazy experiments. What's it to be this time – bladder control by telepathy? I wish you'd never heard of Barbara Woodhouse.'

'It's nothing to do with Barbara Woodhouse, although now you mention it she does say puppies can be trained very early.'

'One of these days the BBC will show the bits they cut out of the Woodhouse films. Dogs peeing over the electric cables, bitches being deflowered off-camera. The failures.'

'Don't be silly. Listen, this other woman – she's a friend of Sue's – tried putting a fresh piece of turf in the puppies' box directly they could walk. Sue said they did all their messes there right from the start. I don't know about their bladders though, I'd have to check with Sue.'

'If you think I'm going to cut up pieces of our lawn each day to provide a pups' loo you've got another think coming. They can go out in the stable like Parsley's other litters.'

'Yes, of course they can at night,' I agreed. 'Parsley must have a rest from them anyway once they're on solids. But during the day I'd like to try this grass-training method. You will build me a playpen for them, won't you – about eight by four?'

'Oh a cage? Yes of course I will. Anything to stop them running round the house.'

He set to and constructed a strong wooden pen which he screwed to the skirting board in one corner of the kitchen. The sides were six inches high which we thought would be high enough but we had reckoned without Pansy's extraordinary intelligence and agility. When she was just two weeks old she accidentally fell out of the box – she was on top of a pyramid of her sleeping siblings and tumbled over the edge when they moved – and after that she worked out for herself how to repeat the trick. All she had to do was to wait until one of the other pups was lying against the six-inch plank then she would use him or her as a stepping-stone to freedom. She was always one stage ahead of the others in her development, being the first to open her eyes, to teethe, and then to walk.

William, the last born and Parsley's favourite, couldn't have been more different. His was such a sweet placid nature I even registered him as Sweet William on his Kennel Club certificate. He distanced himself from his anarchist sisters and brother and would sit watching them with a puzzled expression while they systematically wrecked everything left at floor level. We bought them rubber toys, dumbbells, balls, and a yellow squeaky tortoise and enjoyed hours of entertainment watching them play. The tortoise, almost immediately reduced to a legless, headless blob, was their favourite toy. It made a noise like a puppy and many's the time Brian tripped over it and almost had heart failure thinking he had trodden on a puppy. 'They'll have to go,' became his familiar battle cry, not a very convincing one.

To everybody's surprise the turf-training method worked. The pups became as clean as kittens and used the turf for all their messes. Not their puddles though, I don't know why. We kept a toilet roll near their box and would rush to get it as soon as an accident occurred. One evening we could hardly believe our eyes when Pansy raced out of the sitting room and staggered back in carrying the toilet roll in her mouth. One of the other pups had made a puddle which we hadn't even noticed but evidently Pansy had and was being as helpful as she could. The second time it happened she co-opted William as her porter and made us seriously consider phoning the toilet roll manufacturers to say scrub your labrador puppy adverts, we've got two spaniel pups who know what loo paper is for and don't waste it by unravelling it.

Although Brian would disagree, not every minute of every day was taken up by the puppies. There is no one in the world I envy more than Konrad Lorenz but since nobody was going to pay *me* to record animal behaviour I reluctantly turned my attention back to life in the Garden Centre and the human animals. Their behaviour, while not as captivating as the puppies', would have kept an anthropologist on his toes. Mr Gill for instance. Why did this Pickwickian old boy always talk about Oliver Cromwell?

Mr Gill lived in a chocolate-box cottage half-way between two villages. One village had fought for Cromwell in the Civil War while the other had been Royalists to a man. Mr Gill, though old, was not actually old enough to have been present while the two villages slogged it out, but to hear him talk you got the impression that it had all happened a fortnight ago. Gill himself was a staunch Royalist who had been drawn to our shop not by our fine selection of economically priced plants but because we bred Cavaliers.

He was entranced when I told him that because of an unrepealed act of parliament Cavalier King Charles Spaniels are the only breed of dog allowed by law to enter theatres, opera houses and any other establishment displaying 'No Dogs' notices. 'That's one in the eye for Cromwell,' he said gleefully and in return told us things about Cromwell's personal habits that we didn't know and would have horrified Cromwell's own mother. As well as these interesting tidbits about the great man he also drew our attention to the dissimilarities between the inhabitants of village A and village B. 'Even today,' he said, leaping effortlessly over the centuries, 'you can see the results of in-breeding at B. A terrible tight-knit lot they are, physically deformed, only ninepence in the shilling poor things, whereas A's people are bigger and healthier. Charlie saw to that.'

'What personally?' I pictured King Charles taking time off from state duties to scatter his seed among the milkmaids.

'Probably,' said Mr Gill with a twinkle. 'And certainly his noblemen would have been encouraged to produce little noblepeople even if they were born the wrong side of the blanket. The point is, they were of good stock and as I say you can still see the quality in their descendants.'

School history lessons had never been like this. It was hard to resist the temptation to rush out and conduct a census in both villages in order to test Mr Gill's theory but Brian said if I started knocking on doors asking indiscreet questions I would end up in hospital so I had to content myself with doing my weekly shop in alternate villages and merely observing. I couldn't see much difference in the two sets of inhabitants: B's people were not all 'ninepence in the shilling' nor were A's all lusty specimens but as that village had unlimited parking and no traffic wardens I had no hesitation in remaining loyal to the Cavalier King.

Mr Gill was one of our favourite customers; Mr Goddard was not. He was a damned nuisance from start to finish, a know-all who knew nothing. He was planting a garden from scratch and although we had told him over and over again that we couldn't supply fencing or slabs he hung around pestering until Brian gave him a note to take to the wholesaler's so that he could get a discount for patio materials. Then he was back for peat. Brian assured him that putting peat on reclaimed Dartmoor pasture would be like adding sugar to syrup but no, he had to have peat, a ton of it. Brian tried to talk him into buying it at the Cash and Carry where it was 50p a bag cheaper than ours. He could have been talking to a brick wall. Goddard wanted our peat – 'It must be better quality if it's dearer,' he argued, so Brian ordered and delivered forty ½-cwt bags after which he had to lie down with a hot-water bottle at his back for several hours to recover.

All this was time-consuming and profitless but nothing compared to the next item on Goddard's agenda: rare plants. 'Have you read this book?' he said excitedly one day. 'It's all about rare plants.' Brian and I looked at each other, then at the sky. No deliverance was forthcoming. 'I've marked the ones I want you to order,' Goddard continued and laid the book open on the shop counter.

'Mr Goddard,' said Brian in shocked tones, 'you've written in a library book.'

'Call me Colin,' said Goddard. 'I feel as though I've been coming here for years.'

'Years,' Brian agreed glumly.

But Goddard's skin was thick. 'There are about forty I want you to order for me,' he continued as if we were the greatest friends. 'I've decided to do my bit for conservation. I might even be able to propagate from these in a few years; rather a good cause, don't you think?' He burbled on about seed banks while we leafed through his defaced library book. His knowledge of horticulture had reached the stage where he just about knew which end of a plant was the root. Give him thirty rare plants to nurture and the world would be minus forty rare plants.

Realising it would be useless to dissuade him, Brian made a list of the plants and told Goddard he would see what he could do. If it had been on behalf of anyone else the task of tracing suppliers of rare plants would have been a pleasure but every time he phoned a specialist grower or wrote to Kew Garden experts he knew he was probably sending another plant to its doom.

A week or so later, after exhaustive enquiries, he had managed to trace the growers of all but five of the plants on the list. He phoned Goddard: 'They're expensive, Mr Goddard, so I'm phoning to confirm that you really do want all of them before I send off the orders . . . No, I haven't paid for them yet . . . What do you mean "good"? You've *what*?' He ground his knuckles into the wall by the phone – no prizes for guessing whose face he was pulverising.

'He's changed his mind?' I said. Brian nodded, listened to the voice on the end of the line for a few moments more, then rang off. It was a while before he was coherent enough to put me in the picture and a much longer while before either of us was able to see the funny side of the situation. For Goddard, having ordered a ton of peat didn't want to waste it and had now decided to plant his garden with acid-loving shrubs.

'His choice or ours?' I said.

'Ours.'

'I'll do it. If you have any more dealings with him you'll blow a gasket.'

I consulted Hilliers. Since Goddard wouldn't have known an azalea from a dandelion I thought I would simply stick a pin in the section on acid-tolerant shrubs and he could like or lump whatever I chose. What I didn't choose, even though it was the first thing my pencil landed on, was Elaeocarpaceae Crinodendron Hookerianum. Not for anyone, much less for Goddard, would I attempt to squeeze those words on to plastic labels.

'Give him some of that horrible ilex,' Brian suggested. 'Nobody else will buy it.'

'Brilliant,' I said. 'Only four letters.' I scanned Hilliers again, not caring tuppence whether the selection was varied and interesting. The challenge was to find acid-loving, short-named plants. Acer, Hebe, Ribes . . .

Chapter Nine

'FIRST FROST,' BRIAN reported cheerfully, bringing me a cup of tea in bed.

'Is that good?'

'Of course it's good. It's cleansing. It'll knock out every aphid on the place.'

'I'm not an aphid,' I moaned as he flung the windows open.

'Do get up, it's a lovely day. Bracing.' He breathed in great lungfuls of the lethal oxygen. I picked up my clothes and made a dash for the Rayburn in the kitchen. I don't mind being cleansed or braced but I don't like having it sprung on me.

The first frost heralded the start of a new year, horticulturally speaking. Non-hardy plants succumbing to cold could now be thrown out and sterilisation of beds and greenhouses begun. Running a Garden Centre seemed a bit like running an old folks' home. In both establishments the residents have to be sheltered and fed, visitors made welcome and vacant beds swiftly refilled to ensure a constant cash flow. But at least in our line of business we didn't mind when some of our weaker specimens gave up the ghost; in fact it was quite a relief to be rid of the last of the summer stock and turn our attention to bulbs.

Earlier in the year Brian had buried several hundred prepared (artificially forced) hyacinth bulbs in cold frames under damp peat. Now the time had come to lift them and pot them on ready for the Christmas trade. To my mind there never was a more enjoyable Garden Centre job than potting bulbs. Thanks to Small not one had been attacked by mice and thanks to Brian's meticulous positioning under the peat the whole batch had sprouted evenly. We scrabbled them out of the cold frames with our fingers, being careful not to break any roots, and laid them on trays which we then carried into the propagation house. Brian had been to the wholesaler's and bought some straight-sided, quite nicely designed bowls in plain colours – brown, white and green – and these we filled with bulb fibre and began planting.

'How much are we going to sell these for?' I asked.

'Well, the bulbs were 15p each and we're putting three to a bowl. The bowls cost 30p, the fibre about 10p. Have I forgotten anything?'

'Labour?'

'Oh yes, labour.'

'It's very nice labour, isn't it? We shouldn't really charge much if we're enjoying it.'

Brian said he hoped I would never become a member of a trade union and went back to his sums. 'Where was I? 85p plus a bit for ribbon and moss. We can sell them for £1.30 each.'

Throughout the day customers wandered into the propagating house and some, seeing what we were doing, wanted to help. Gardeners are an odd lot, they're never happier than when their fingernails are full of soil. There is a scene in *Tom Sawyer* where Tom, tired of creosoting his aunt's fence, pretends he is enjoying it and soon has his friends queuing up, begging to be allowed to have a turn. If we had wanted to I'm sure we could have delegated the bulb planting in the same way. But nobody was allowed to lay a finger on our hyacinths until right at the end, when there were just a few odd ones left, we let a woman plant them in single pots. I don't know who she was but she said she was killing time while her son was sitting an entrance exam at a near-by school. She explored the propagating house and asked Brian why he kept a box of fireworks on the bench. 'They're not fireworks,' Brian said, 'they're smoke bombs. You shut all the doors and ventilators then light one. It fumigates all the crevices you can't get into with a brush and leaves the whole area germ-free.'

'Oh,' she said in surprise, 'what a splendid idea. I wonder if I could get one for my son's bedroom.'

Within a week the robust little hyacinth spears had greened up and the bowls were ready for mossing. In London when we had had the flowershop we used to have to buy bun moss and very expensive it was too. But here in the foothills of Dartmoor it grew in profusion, great sheets of it clinging to immense granite boulders. After getting permission from the landowners to take it, I spent hours collecting it in plastic carrier bags which I slung over the ponies' saddles. I could have taken the van but it was much more fun doing it on horseback. Rory, now that he had done his basic training, turned out to be a useful pack pony as he seldom wanted to go faster than a walk; also he was the sort of pony you could leave untethered. I would simply knot the reins over his neck and leave him to nibble the undergrowth while I peeled the bun moss off the boulders with a plasterer's trowel and a penknife. When my bags were full, all I had to do was call him and he would amble back to me like a rather slow-witted dog. But if I took Noah on a collecting expedition I didn't dare turn him loose or he would have hot-footed it across the moor.

Noah's native intelligence stood us in good stead one day. He and I, after moss collecting, had wandered about a mile off the beaten track on the high moor itself when suddenly a thick mist enveloped us. I had read about Dartmoor mists but I had no idea how frightening they can be. Visibility was literally no more than ten feet and there was a deadening silence all round us. Worst of all it was cold, really cold. I whistled the dogs and they materialised out of nowhere, their fur beaded with droplets of moisture. 'We're lost,' I told them. They wagged their tails. 'Go home?' I tried hopefully but the last thing they wanted to do was go home when they were having such an interesting walk.

I believe there are some clever people, ex-Biggles readers probably, who can navigate by the hands of a watch. I looked at my watch – crikey was that the time? It would be dark in an hour. I tightened Noah's girth, mounted and set off in what I hoped was a straight line. It was eerie not to be able to see where we were going and positively scary to think we might be knee-deep in bog any minute. Brian would be so cross – 'How many times have I told you to take a *compass*' he'd say. Maybe the bogs were so deep we would sink without trace and lie there preserved in peat until archaeologists dug us up in a million years' time. I found the idea alarming but curiously attractive; I picked Parsley up and let her ride on the saddle in front of me. Now the archaeologists would uncover a still more touching tableau – a family of pets, one still clasped protectively in the arms of its owner . . .

Noah, finding his head free – I couldn't control him and Parsley at the same time – wheeled round and started to go back the way we had come. 'Hoy Noah, what are you doing?' I said, then I remembered that moorland ponies have a highly developed sense of direction across open country.

As surely as a homing pigeon Noah took us across the blackened heather, carefully skirting round those sinister emerald areas that denote bogs, and twenty minutes later his hooves were clattering on a stony well-worn path. I still didn't know quite where we were but the fog was thinner lower down and I could see one or two familiar landmarks.

'You're late back,' Brian said as we trooped in.

'I know. A fog came down and we got lost.'

'Where?'

'If I knew where I wouldn't have been lost, would I? It was somewhere up on the moor.'

'You shouldn't go on the moor without a compass, some of the bogs are dodgy. Did you get enough moss to finish the bowls?'

The finished bowls made a gorgeous display in one of the polytunnels. As is usual with hyacinths the blue ones opened first, then the white, yellow and pink all together. They smelt good, they looked marvellous with matching ribbon bow nestling in the moss and they were excellent value for £1.30. But they didn't sell very well. We had grown too many for our regular customers to buy up and as people tend to shop in towns during the winter we had hardly any casual trade. One or two customers coming in for potting compost or Baby Bio said: 'Oh I *wish* I'd known you were selling planted bowls for £1.30. I paid over two pounds in town and they weren't nearly as good as yours,' which was cold comfort.

Brian took a vanload round local village greengrocers and gift shops but by Christmas we still had dozens left. All but distant friends received hyacinths for Christmas presents and those that we had left – hyacinths not friends – adorned every windowsill in the house.

Marcus and Sara came home for the holiday together with Sara's latest boyfriend, an emotional Italian lad who wanted to marry her. He regaled us with tales of his grandmother, a very old lady who dressed in black and who was 'into death' as Luigi put it. According to Luigi, Gran spent her days eagerly scanning obituary columns and attending memorial services, sometimes of complete strangers if Gran liked the look of the church and if none of her own acquaintances had obliged.

We quite liked Luigi; he repaired one of Brian's grass cutters that a local garage had given up on, and he was dotty about Sara. His effect on her was rather disconcerting though. One evening we all went out to a local hotel for a meal. Over pre-dinner drinks I looked out of the window and saw an escaped pig running around the hotel car park. Automatically Brian, Marcus and I rushed out and helped capture and re-pen the animal. When we returned to the bar I said crossly to Sara: 'Why didn't you come and help?' and she said she didn't want to ruin her new Italian sandals. I couldn't believe my ears – a daughter of mine putting shoes before pigs? 'That's your influence,' I said to Luigi.

'Don't start on him,' Sara said, 'he hasn't done anything.' Luigi wisely said nothing but looked a bit bewildered as we filed into the dining room.

Marcus, having unaccountably become a vegan, lectured us all on cannibalism as we tucked into meat and two veg. His own meal he subjected to pathological investigation, peering closely at every nut and lentil before deigning to eat it. But when the sweet trolley came round he abandoned his principles and enjoyed some positively non-vegan pudding 'But no cream thanks, there are limits.'

'Go on,' I said, 'be a devil. This is the last square meal you'll have for months.' He was planning a hitch-hiking trip round India with a friend and would be off in a few days.

113

'No really,' he said. 'I've got to train myself to live frugally.' We all roared with laughter as Marcus is famous for his thrift.

'Who uses tea bags twice?' Sara taunted.

'I don't drink tea any more and neither should you. Caffeine— '

'Stop being so pompous,' said Brian. 'I'm going to ask the waitress for some caffeine-rich coffee. What will you have, Marcus?'

'Would you mind if I just had a glass of hot water?'

'Of course I don't mind. Could we have coffee for four please and a glass of hot water,' he said to the waitress.

'And a spoon, please,' Marcus added.

'Marcus – you *haven't*,' I said when the waitress had gone.

'I have. Why not? I don't drink coffee.' He fished a herbal tea bag out of his pocket.

'Put it away,' Brian groaned. 'You'll get us thrown out.'

Looking round at the rest of the diners I wondered if any of the other family groups included daughters with strange values and sons on strange diets. It was heartening to see a couple remonstrating with a punk daughter; we had been spared that phase. Sara's hair sometimes looked as if she had styled it by putting two wet fingers into a live electric socket but she had never wanted studs in her nose or anything like that, and Marcus of course had far too much regard for his organically-reared body to risk putting dyes or ornaments anywhere near it.

The youngsters went back to London in time for New Year's Eve ongoings combined with sending-Marcus-and-Vernon-to-India parties. (Vernon was the boy Marcus set out with but he returned to England after a couple of months of Marcus's vegan sermons.) After a flying visit from some friends we declared Christmas over and got down to work again.

The last batch of planted bowls were now eagerly snapped up. Minus their ribbon bows they made ideal sympathy gifts for the recently bereaved. As every florist and Luigi's grandmother knows, early January is the peak time for being 'into death'. Our London flowershop had been next door to an undertaker's; their hearses were always occupied in January, especially after snow or a flu epidemic.

The pattern of the previous year repeated itself in that the roof started leaking again and the cheerful young builders reoccupied their old nesting site. We had changed to Eagle Star insurance by now and found them very satisfactory. Not only did they pay for the roof repairs, they even offered to pay for interior decoration where necessary. Brian told them it wasn't necessary as only one wall had been ruined and we had kept back several rolls of wallpaper for this sort of emergency. To our amazement they asked for the wallpaper receipt and when we sent it they insisted on paying twelve pounds towards it as a goodwill gesture.

The builders, who had a lovely view of the surrounding countryside when they weren't thawing out in the kitchen, asked me why I didn't provide cream teas for our summer customers. 'You've got a smashing lawn, Mrs A, people would enjoy sitting there looking at the view after they'd been round all the plants.'

They were not the only ones to make this suggestion. Heaps of summer customers had already asked where they could get tea and Addy had been urging me to start cream teas and morning coffee for years. I had resisted, saying that it wouldn't be a very profitable venture now that we no longer had a cow, a thin excuse even to my ears.

'I don't want to go in for catering,' I said to Brian when he was making lists of possible sidelines we could start in the holiday season.

'Don't then. But I think we'll have to provide seating for people this year. They look so untidy when they drape themselves round the car park.'

'They do,' I agreed. 'And I'm always being asked to fetch chairs for old ladies. It's their feet.'

Brian wrote 'Seats – uncomfortable'.

'Why uncomfortable?'

'Because people sitting down are people not spending money.'

'But' – I could see the trap looming in front of me but seemed powerless to avoid it – 'if they're sitting down drinking tea they *would* be spending money.'

Brian wrote 'Cream teas'.

Shortly after this one of our customers, a sweet old lady with excellent feet, gave me the name and address of someone who 'knew all about' cream teas. 'Sylvia will give you lots of advice,' she said. 'She's a saint.'

'A saint?' I said in horror. 'Holy water and blessings?'

The old lady laughed. 'Not that sort of saint, a down to earth sort. She's got a pony sanctuary.'

In less time than it takes to tell I was in the van and on my way to meet St Sylvia. I had shouted to Brian on the way out 'Just going to see a woman about cream teas' and now giggled to myself wondering what on earth he must have thought of my apparent eagerness to learn about catering.

'If it's jumble, stick it in the garage,' a voice called out as I drove into the stable yard of the Devon Horse and Pony Sanctuary. A woman of about my own age backed out of a loose-box in the manner that every animal owner would recognise and shut the lower half of the door smartly: 'You stay there you old devil, it's only for ten minutes.'

'What are you shutting in?' I asked.

'Lamby. She pinches the ponies' feed if I don't stop her.'

'Can I see?' I looked over the stable door expecting to see a lamb. A sheep the size of a buffalo frowned up at me through a thick woolly topknot. 'Lamby?' I said. 'For a thing that size?'

'She started off as a lamb. The name sort of stuck.'

'They do, don't they,' I agreed. 'We had a sweet little lamb once called Ramrod. Then he became a stud ram and we wished we'd called him something else. Are you Sylvia?'

We introduced ourselves and Sylvia said, 'Oh, you're the couple that bought the run-down nursery, are you? What a dump – that bungalow should be bulldozed.'

'We're going to paint it sludge green so that it's not quite such an eyesore,' I said, taking an instant liking to a fellow anti-Bung. Lamby butted the stable door and Sylvia said: 'Don't go away. I'll just feed the hooligans, then Lamby can come out again.' She placed six feeding bowls in a line and crossed the yard to open a field gate. Six shaggy young ponies stampeded to the food and after a brief tussle to see who was going to have which bowl they all lowered their heads and began to eat. While they were occupied Sylvia lugged a bale of hay from a near-by stack. 'Good job you've come in wellingtons,' she grinned as we carried the bale out to the paddock and distributed it into piles.

After the ponies had eaten their hard feed and returned to their paddock Sylvia released Lamby to hoover up the few stray oats remaining in the bowls. 'That's the lot,' she said. 'Do you want to have a look round?'

The sanctuary ponies – eighteen on the premises and twelve outwintered – were divided into age and personality groups. First there were the orphan foals, bottle-fed and bedded on thick straw. They were so enchanting, these foal-de-rols as Sylvia called them, that I had the greatest difficulty in tearing myself away to see the next group, the delinquents. These were new arrivals who, for one reason or another, mistrusted humans. They would live in a securely fenced small yard for a few weeks, receiving nothing but food and reassurance several times a day, until their terrors had subsided enough for them to be handled. Then they would either be promoted to the hooligan group – unbroken colts and fillies – or, if they needed equine counselling, placed under the wing of an experienced middle-aged mare, Dolly. (Dolly also pulled a wagon, giving outings to handicapped children who were part of the Riding for the Disabled scheme.)

When the animals reached adulthood the peer groups were changed to personality groups. One old donkey had chosen to live with a goat, while a tall horse had become so smitten by a Shetland pony that he went off his food until they were allowed to live together. I met the geriatrics last. We spent longer with them, readjusting their warm rugs and stroking their necks; it was plain to see these were Sylvia's favourites. One of them still bore the scars from floggings it had received when it worked in a riding school.

'Have you got time for a cup of tea?' Sylvia asked as we strolled back to the house.

'Tea – oh heck, I'd forgotten. That's what I came for.'

'What, tea?' said Sylvia in surprise. 'Why didn't you say so before? It won't take a moment to put the kettle on.'

'No, cream teas for holidaymakers. I'm thinking of doing it and one of our customers told me you could give me some tips. She said you were a saint.'

Sylvia laughed. We kicked our wellies off in the porch and went into a dog-filled kitchen. Over tea Sylvia told me how she and her husband had started the sanctuary by rescuing a forty-five-year-old mare from a fate a lot worse than death. 'She was being hired out for a pound an hour.'

'At *forty-five*?' I gasped.

'I don't suppose the riders were told how old she was. All they knew was that she didn't go very fast unless she was thrashed. Anyway, we had a café at the time – that's where we did the cream teas incidentally – but we didn't have any grazing. So we sold the business in order to buy some land for the poor old girl and before we knew what was happening horses and ponies came flooding in.'

'And sheep?'

'And sheep and donkeys and goats. It's so hard to refuse, isn't it?'

'How can you afford to feed them all?'

'It's not easy. We're a registered charity so we're able to do the usual things, jumble sales, collecting boxes and so on but we're always broke. At the moment we're desperate for more New Zealand rugs and a new stable block.'

'I'll try and find you an animal-loving millionaire,' I promised, then reluctantly returned to the purpose of my visit. Sylvia reeled off everything she could remember about cream teas from planning permission to the quality of the spoons. I filled three notebook pages as she talked and felt exhausted at the apparent complications involved in serving a simple snack to a bunch of holidaymakers.

'You'll find they're mostly very easy to please,' said Sylvia, 'much the same as your Garden Centre customers, I imagine. The ones I couldn't stand were the toffee-nosed families, you know the sort – the ones that give their kids stupid names like Marcus and Peregrine.'

'My son's called Marcus.'

'Is he? I expect he was horrible when he was small, all Marcuses are. But as I was saying, most of your customers will be OK. You won't be able to avoid Germans of course, not in Devon, but even Germans have their advantages at the tea table.'

'What advantages?'

She smiled at some private joke. 'I'll let you find out for yourself, it'll be a nice surprise. Now I wonder if I've left anything out?'

I looked at my notes. 'I don't seem to have anything about costing here. How much shall I charge?'

'Eighty-five pence. That's twenty-five cheaper than most other tea places and if you're not too hasty with their change they'll leave the odd fifteen as a tip.'

It was dark by the time I got home and my own ponies were in no mood to listen to my sentimental account of ill-treated ponies finding peace in a sanctuary. They pawed impatiently on the fodder-room door and whickered, – What time do you call this? *Wasting away* we are – and when the food appeared they barged past me like Sylvia's hooligan colts.

'It's a lovely place,' I told Brian at supper. 'All the animals are so happy. I wish I could have a sanctuary. There was this black mare called Heidi with a foal called Paul and you'll never guess what Paul did. He— '

Brian said if I didn't shut up and concentrate on our own business we would shortly find we were in need of a sanctuary ourselves. 'The *cream teas*,' he persisted. 'What did she tell you about cream teas?'

'Lots. I wrote it all down.' I passed him my notebook and waited for him to congratulate me on my in-depth research. He read it carefully. 'It's gibberish,' he said. 'What on earth is p.p. R and p.p. Loo?'

'That's to do with planning permission. You have to have planning permission for refreshments – R means refreshments – but you might not get it unless you have a separate lavatory. The trouble is you have to deal with a different department to get planning permission for a loo.'

119

'We can't afford a second loo. What does this bit mean – German surprise?'

'I don't know.'

'But you wrote it.'

'It's going to be a surprise.'

'And PHD? Not ponies horses donkeys I hope.'

'Public Health Dept. It's obvious.'

'It's totalling baffling. Why don't you put your notes in columns with proper headings?'

'Don't worry, I can understand what I've written. The teas won't be any problem once I've sorted out the planning permission. Can you make some tables and seating for twenty? Rustic benches would look rather nice, wouldn't they?'

The cost of the wood to make bench-style tables and seats was so astronomical we had to abandon that idea and settle for second-hand wooden tables and folding chairs. I wanted to sand and varnish the tables but Brian said the wood wasn't good enough so I painted them instead. Parsley's puppies helped and Brian's refrain 'They'll have to go' reached fever pitch.

'Blenheim Cavaliers for sale' my low-key advert started. No matter how many times you sell a litter of puppies it never gets any easier to part with them. You can hope the ad won't be read or that all the prospective buyers will be so unsuitable you can say No with a clear conscience. Snuff had already gone, to a first-rate home – Garden Centre customers who had asked if I would mind having him back when they went on holiday. So that left four.

It was not easy to say no to an eighty-year-old woman who wanted to buy William but it had to be done. I tried every way I could think of but my message wasn't getting through. 'I'm sorry,' I said at last, 'but a puppy is for ten or twelve years. You might not live that long.' It was an awful thing to say but not as awful as the thought of William grieving for a dead owner.

There were one or two other hiccups before all the puppies had been compatibly homed; Polly to Somerset, William to a seaside family and Poppy and Pansy to a herb farm in Dorset.

This was one home where I could be certain that their perfect health would be maintained. No vaccinations, no tinned food and no refined cereals. Lucky pups.

(Pansy grew up into a great individualist with an intelligence to match. An example of the way she figured things out is the remarkable story of how she *sold one of her own puppies*. She broke out of her garden one day and wandered up and down pretending to be lost until a kind woman passing by read the address on her collar and took her home. The majority of people can resist a basketful of fat puppies but Pansy's sixth sense hadn't let her down. The woman looked at the puppies and bought one on the spot.)

Being puppyless wasn't as bad as usual. Snuff would be coming back for his holiday and we would be seeing William from time to time when his owners came to buy plants. And being puppyless was essential if we were to pass the public health inspection for catering. They won't even consider a place if they suspect dogs or cats live in the kitchen.

Optimistically (for the builders were still on the roof and one never knew where they would channel rainwater next) we decorated the kitchen. Removing old paint from metal window frames with wire brushes must rate as one of the worst D.I.Y. jobs there is. That horrible noise of metal on metal; it makes my teeth ache just thinking about it.

Previous occupants had not bothered to strip either paint or paper but had simply put fresh layers of both over the old. We counted five different sorts of wallpaper laid one on top of another and invented people to match the patterns; a rather anaemic lot, except for one Hinge and Bracket couple who had daringly allowed the odd rosebud to creep into the decor. Our own taste of course wouldn't please everyone; we tend to like bright colours. A close friend once described a room of ours as a mixed grill and when we stood back and looked at it objectively we could see how *she* saw fried eggs in some of the yellow pattern.

With the health inspector in mind we played safe and chose white paintwork and a white and green wallpaper for the kitchen. It looked like an illustration out of a dental journal when we had finished and we hated it. So Brian went off to town and had the paint shop mix him up some polyurethane gloss in an emphatic shade of red.

'*Strewth*,' I said when he opened the tin.

'Don't you like it? It's called Rosy Glow.'

'I love it. It's not a rosy glow though – more like House on Fire.'

We tried it out on a piece of wood and held it up to the light. Then, because we were sick to death of the characterless bungalow and because we craved colour in the dead of winter, we dipped our brushes in and painted all the cupboard fronts with it.

It was sensational. Rudolf Steiner would have been gratified to see the way we cheered up after this orgy of colour had been applied. I cleaned the Rayburn which promptly went out, from shock probably, and Brian polished the windows. We were ready for the health inspector.

Chapter Ten

LIVING INSIDE THE boundary of Dartmoor National Park meant seeking permission from the Park authorities as well as the council before we could serve refreshments. They were not concerned with public health or customers' car parks but with advertising signs. Their rules were straightforward enough: no signs over a certain height, no flashing signs or psychedelic colours or anything else that might detract from the scenery. We thoroughly approved of rules like these and said so when the Park's enforcement officer came to look at our tea signs. He was much too nice to be anything as fierce-sounding as an enforcement officer. His name was Peter and he was an enthusiastic walker as Brian discovered within minutes of meeting him. They nattered on about maps and walks they had done or wanted to do and the awfulness of tourists who used Dartmoor as a litter bin.

'If you don't allow silly signs,' I said as soon as I could get a word in edgeways, 'why have you let someone put a Jesus Saves poster next to that cattle grid on the moor?' This was a particular thorn in my flesh as the poster in question had been stuck on a garden wall not twenty yards from the body of a run-over sheep.

'It's not advertising,' Peter explained, 'and there's not much we can do about it unless someone complains.' I said I was complaining on behalf of the sheep but apparently proxy complaints didn't count. Our own signs – Cream Teas and Coffee – in four-inch black letters on a white background were a form of advertising but of such a modest nature they posed no threat to the scenery. Peter had a cup of tea with us and departed, no forms no fuss – a perfect example of how bureaucracy should work.

In complete contrast, the local council sent men and forms

galore but we had had some experience of this game before and managed to short-circuit a lot of their nit-picking procedures. The best way of dealing with forms, we had discovered, is to keep sending them back. Nobody ever actually reads them but they do like to have them so all you do is fill them in – it doesn't matter much what you put – and return them. One particularly bizarre question on a duplicated form relating to the proposed new lavatory was: 'For what purpose will the building be used?' and just for fun we put 'For stirring the scone-mix' on one and 'Additional seating' on the other.

One department had a penchant for drawings. This presented a problem since neither of us can draw. We had a stab at an aerial viewpoint of our property with arrows signifying the parts we proposed to set aside for the refreshment areas. Unfortunately the forms were in quadruplicate so the fourth drawing didn't look anything like the first one and they sent them back. They also sent back our four drawings of a lavatory with 'unacceptable' stamped on them. I was quite offended as I had painstakingly drawn four WC pans on separate pieces of paper and was proud of my efforts. I thought they looked Picasso-ish blocked in with two shades of blue felt tip.

'They want proper plans,' said Brian, reading the accompanying letter. 'Draughtsmen's drawings.'

'We don't know any draughtsmen *and* they'd be expensive. Why don't we drop the whole idea?' It seemed absurd to be wasting our time on these endless forms for a loo we couldn't afford.

'What about Sara's architect friend?' Brian suggested. 'He might be able to draw some plans cheaply.'

'We could ask Sara to ask him,' I said doubtfully, 'but I'm sure architects don't work on anything as small as an outside loo.'

Sara had recently moved into a mixed sex flat share in St Johns Wood. One of the other tenants was a thirty-five-year-old architect called Dominic. We had been a little apprehensive about the set-up but Sara told us firmly that we were living in the Dark Ages. Nobody else's parents worried about mixed sharing, good heavens what did we imagine a man of thirty-five could get up to? Brian said he had heard of some thirty-five-year-olds who still had some of their faculties left but Sara dismissed this as 'probably boasting'.

Dominic was approached and agreed to draw up some simple plans which would comply with building regulations. I wrote to the council telling them that the drawings would be forthcoming as soon as our architect had completed them and, improbable as it sounds, this last letter closed the correspondence. Dominic never got round to doing the drawings so the council never had anything except my rejected Picassos. It must have been the magic 'our architect' that made them approve of us to the extent of passing us along the line to Public Health.

Public Health sent a different man from the one who had eaten our coloured powders. This one was extremely friendly and, unlike his suicidal colleague, in no hurry to dash back to his test tubes. Before he came I had driven the dogs over to my mother's for the day and locked Small in a bedroom. There wasn't a trace of dog or cat in the kitchen, in fact there wasn't a trace of anything much so thoroughly had I cleaned up. ('Bare in here' was the builders' opinion. They had promised to stay quietly on the roof and not play their radio during the inspector's visit.)

'*What* a nice kitchen,' Public Health enthused. 'Have you been here long?' He sat down at the table and I made a pot of tea for two. Brian, whose earthy appearance marked him down as a health hazard, had been banished along with the dogs. When the tea was brewed I carried it to the table on a tray with a snowy white tray cloth. We had had a full dress rehearsal the day before.

P.H. asked me all sorts of questions about the new venture – where would I prepare the food, how big was my freezer, did I know about not storing meat and milk together, what did I know about the decomposition rate of clotted cream in hot weather – all elementary stuff. I would have liked him to ask me questions on the life-cycle of the bluebottle as it's a subject I have studied in depth but we didn't get around to bluebottles except in general terms. He told me some hair-raising tales about hotel kitchens, then he got up and prowled around looking in cupboards and drawers.

'You have a very satisfactorily ordered kitchen,' he said and I could have kissed him. Nobody has ever said anything like that to me before. He looked down the plughole in the sink and behind the fridge and freezer. Electric plugs, baking trays, crockery, saucepans, everything was minutely examined and replaced.

'Splendid,' he said at last. 'If everyone had a kitchen like yours I'd be out of a job.'

'You'll pass us for cream teas then?'

'Yes, I think so. There's just one thing – when did you last have your water tested?'

I stared at him for a moment before cottoning on.

'Oh, the tap water. About six months ago. My husband cleaned out the well, then we had the water analysed to be on the safe side.'

'A well?' He was suddenly expectant, like a gun dog scenting a rabbit. 'I didn't know you had a well.'

'It's not a real well, we just call it that because it sounds nicer than holding tank or reservoir, doesn't it? The water comes from a flooded tin mine higher up.'

'Oh yes,' he said. He seemed disappointed that he hadn't discovered a well full of floating cats. 'I remember now – this valley is in a tin belt, isn't it? They flooded a lot of the old workings when they stopped mining early in the century. I'd better see the analyst's report while I'm here but I know what it will say.'

Translated into lay terms the analyst's report said you'd have a job to find a purer sample of water. The odd atom of some trace element or other only enhanced its quality.

'Thoroughbred water, isn't it?' I said.

'It is indeed. Now I must be off.' He gathered up his papers and put his gloves on. 'I wish you every success with your cream teas. Let's hope we have a hot summer.'

As soon as his car was out of sight the builders shivered into the kitchen and stood rubbing their hands over the Rayburn. 'Cor, we thought he was never going, Mrs A. Any tea left in that pot or did he drink it all?'

'You were very good,' I said. 'Put the kettle on and make some fresh, would you? I'll go and tell my husband he can come in now.'

Before long the dogs and Small plus their baskets and toys were back in their accustomed places and the satisfactorily ordered kitchen just a memory. 'It *did* look civilised,' Brian said wistfully.

'Go on, Mr A,' said one of the lads. 'It didn't look like a place to live in. I wouldn't fancy a place without pets myself. Ever thought about having a monkey, Mrs A? My mum won't let me have a monkey but I'd like one if I get married and have a place of my own.'

'We have *never* thought about having a monkey,' Brian said through gritted teeth and he sent the boys home before I'd even thought of lending them some Gerald Durrell books.

Seed sowing, pricking out and potting on started in earnest as the days lengthened. We were much more experienced now and able to work at twice the speed of the first year. One of the ways we saved time was in buying ready-bagged potting composts. Previously we had mixed our own in a pit using ordinary garden spades to turn it but the work had been back-breaking and only saved a few pence per pot. With the bagged stuff, all you had to do was heave it on to a bench, slit open the polythene, and there it was ready for use at just the right consistency.

There were very few customers as the ground was too hard and too cold to work so we were both free to get on with the greenhouse jobs. Even on the coldest days it was cosy in the propagation house; with an electric kettle and Radio 4 we were very contented and even managed to be polite to the occasional customer who ran us to earth.

'Here you are – naughty people,' said one, letting in an icy blast as she opened the door.

'Ssh,' we chorused. The afternoon play was just ending and it was a good one. The customer who was small and fat scrambled on to a high stool and sat there with her little legs swinging like a child's until the play ended and Brian switched the radio off.

'The young man on the roof told me where you were, naughty people hiding yourselves in here.' She hopped off the stool and smacked Brian playfully. I moved along the bench to give her more room to manoeuvre. 'Have you seen the new Sutton's catalogue?' she went on. 'It's full of lovely lovely pictures.'

I bit my lip to stop myself laughing and slipped out of the door, leaving Brian looking like a cornered animal lumbered, not for the first time, with a case of catalogue-to-the-head. It wasn't uncommon, the sumptuous illustrations seemed to cause the sap to rise in some women. This one, if she ran true to form, would enjoy a January fantasy of being a cross between Lady Chatterley and Gertrude Jekyll then, later in the year when she had cooled down a bit, she would toddle off quite happily with a few trays of alyssum and lobelia.

There was another woman, a widow with a pocket handkerchief of a garden, who had suddenly decided that as her cottage was called 'Redwood' she would plant a redwood tree next to her plastic fish pond. This would have been fine if she had chosen one of the red-barked Cornus but no, she had been to visit her married daughter in America and had come home with big American ideas. She wanted a Sequoia Sempervirens commonly called Californian Redwood – the largest tree in the world. Brian told her that even if he could get one it would grow so big (over a hundred yards tall) it would undermine the foundations of her cottage. She didn't believe him. She had a theory that as England is smaller than America, root growth is somehow restricted. 'Look at carp,' she argued. 'Everyone knows that they only grow as big as their tank allows.'

'Couldn't you change the name of your cottage?' Brian pleaded. 'Honeysuckle Cottage or Rose Cottage?'

'Myrtle, Bay Tree, Camellia, Acacia,' I said supportively.

Brian flashed me a grateful look. 'Bay Tree – that's a very pretty name.' We had two bay trees outgrowing their pots.

'I'm determined to have a redwood,' she insisted. 'Everybody should plant a tree for posterity. You make some enquiries and let me know.'

After our ordeal with the ghastly Goddard and his rare plants we did no such thing and we heard nothing more from her for some weeks. By then she had read a book with 'Tamarisk' in the title and thought it would be lovely to re-name her cottage 'Tamarisk' with a tree to match. It was pure luck that Brian was unable to buy a tamarisk at that time because she went away for another holiday and came back with a yen for mimosa . . .

One day towards the end of January we were engrossed in one of our potting sessions in the greenhouse when our attention was caught by a talk on 'Woman's Hour'. An anthropologist was telling of a primitive tribe she had discovered in some remote jungle, the nearest thing to the missing-link theory so far. It seemed these sub-people had evolved into rather peculiar beings. For a start they were totally disorganised, aimlessly wandering from spot to spot, eating if food was easily available and going without if it wasn't. They weren't intelligent enough to plan ahead for a rainy day or to construct lasting shelters. The tribe was undoubtedly going to die out, said the anthropologist, because they were so extraordinarily lazy. Some of them had mastered the art of using simple tools but again their lack of responsibility meant it was unlikely that they would bother to pass the knowledge on. They communicated by signs and grunts and were dirty to the point where it endangered their health. Their hair especially was long and verminous.

Brian and I listened to the talk open-mouthed. This was no rare tribe the anthropologist had discovered, this was the British teenager.

'I *must* write to "Woman's Hour",' I said and dashed indoors while the talk was still fresh in my memory. Jotting down a list of the points the speaker had made I drew parallels with each one. The simple tools – bread knife and tin-opener; long dirty hair, laziness, lack of responsibility; yes, it was all there, the hallmarks of bed-sit youngsters in North West

London. Most of all, the grunt language. Who hasn't phoned a friend's number and tried in vain to get the teenage caveman who answers the phone to deliver a message to his mother?

The species is *not* rare, I told 'Woman's Hour', and gave examples of sightings in certain watering holes and Social Security offices in London. I concluded by saying it was a pity the speaker thought these sub-men were unlikely to develop into more effective people, as their mothers rather hoped they would.

Two days later they read my letter on 'Woman's Hour'. I was 'a listener in Devon' and I got quite a kick out of being anonymously famous for a few seconds. It encouraged me to unearth a piece of writing I had completed years ago and take a fresh look at it to see if it was publishable.

It was scarcely legible, let alone publishable. Green mould had formed over the pages, many of which were stuck together with damp. 'Are we harvesting penicillin?' Brian wanted to know.

'It's the thing I wrote about the children's holidays. It's gone bad.'

'Don't let it anywhere near the greenhouses – it looks catching. What are you going to do with it?'

A good question. I first wrote it intending it as an article for the *Lady* or similar magazine but somehow I never managed to keep it short enough. I kept adding fresh bits until it ended up long enough for an entire book. Then (and this was four years ago) I had sent it to a publisher who had kept it for *four months* before sending it back with an accompanying letter nearly as long as the manuscript. The letter struck me as being extremely sniffy and patronising and was full of jargon that a building surveyor might use which I didn't understand. Things like structural alterations, the length of passages and 'tightening'. (How do you tighten a manuscript – put a rubber-band round it?) I had thrown away their letter and consigned what I still thought of as my article to a cupboard.

Normally I don't subscribe to the theory 'if at first you don't succeed, etc.' I think if you don't succeed at first you may as well give up and start something else. But there was something about this record of the two and a half years we spent running children's holidays which made me think it might be interesting to someone, not the firm of backward readers but maybe another publisher.

I phoned an old family friend, a retired writer called Wally. 'I wonder if you'd mind having a look at something I've written? I don't quite know what to do with it.'

'How long is it?'

I looked at the last page. 'Eight hundred pages.'

There was a pause. 'What sort of a something?' said Wally.

'Well it started off as an article about the kids' holidays. I got sort of carried away – you know how it is.'

'Yes I do,' said Wally understandingly. He had a lifetime's professional experience behind him, books, plays and TV scripts ranging from 'Dixon of Dock Green' to 'The Avengers'. 'Send me the first couple of chapters. I may be able to tell you if it's saleable.'

I did so and a few days later he sent a postcard: 'Good, despite the gangrene. Send the rest.' It wouldn't all go in one envelope so I parcelled it up in brown paper and nearly fainted at the post office counter when they said it would cost six pounds. For of course I had to send another six pounds to Wally for return postage. 'You can't become a writer,' Brian said. 'We can't afford it.'

Wally liked the book – it had now definitely hatched from article to book – but agreed with the patronising publishers that alterations were needed. 'A damp course for a start,' he joked in his letter, then getting down to brass tacks he listed all the things that needed to be done. It was too long for a commercial proposition, 65,000 words was what publishers liked not 125,000, so I would have to do some hard pruning. Secondly it started and finished in the wrong places, the first and last chapters could be ditched with advantage. Thirdly, it would have to be typed; handwritten manuscripts were totally unacceptable unless they were undiscovered ones by Shakespeare. It seemed to me, reading Wally's invaluably helpful letter, that the only thing I wouldn't have to alter was the title. He liked *The Year of the Cornflake*.

In the months that followed I often wished I had stopped at that letter to 'Woman's Hour' and not embarked on anything as ambitious as a book. The shortening process was a horrible job, not, as I had imagined, dividing the tome in half but actually rewriting every single paragraph. And there wasn't time to do it in one uninterrupted chunk, there was far too much Garden Centre work for that. Once more the manuscript was put aside to be brought out in fits and starts on rainy days during the summer when there weren't many customers.

Preparations for the cream-tea sideline were well under way. The tables and chairs were stored in a shed and my brand new pass-card to a wholesale caterer's was burning a hole in my pocket. We planned to start during the Easter holidays, outside if the weather was good enough and in the conservatory if it was cold.

The conservatory, still with its Indian restaurant wallpaper and huge stretches of grubby glass, cried out for a facelift; it was so sordid we decided to strip right back to the plaster, re-line the walls and paint the whole thing white. On the day we started there was a short spell of sunshine and this woke up about a million small flies which had evidently been hibernating behind the wallpaper and in the window-frame cracks. It was revolting and if the health inspector had seen it he would have had heart failure. I wanted Brian to use one of his fumigation bombs but he thought we'd better not as the place was going to be for humans not plants. He sprayed the air with a household fly-killer while I hoovered up corpses by the thousand. When we had finished we both felt so dirty we had to have baths which seemed odd as we were only going to get dirty again with the decorating.

'There's something about flies I can't stand,' Brian said, towelling his hair.

'Mm, specially in winter. If we had a bat or two living in the conservatory we wouldn't have flies.'

'Bat droppings in the customers' sugar bowls. It's original. I don't like it but it's original. Come on, let's get started.'

It was a quick and rewarding job. We bonfired the old wallpaper, then painted everything white. When the paint was dry we cleaned the windows, laid a carpet and stuck a few posters on the walls.

'I'm not letting the public in here,' I said. 'It's much too good. Doesn't it look huge?'

'You should be able to seat twenty easily. Shall we try it out?'

'What, bring the tables in now? I don't really want to spoil the look of it. Perhaps *one* table – we could have our meals here.'

'We haven't gone to all this trouble just to give ourselves a dining room. This is for your customers.' He grumbled on but had to admit it was a waste to keep a south-facing conservatory reserved for rainy day tea parties. Soon a plant or two appeared on the ledges, then another and another and it was my turn to grumble. 'You're using it as an annexe for the greenhouses. I don't mind the pots of polyanthus but those trays of tomato seedlings can go back to the prop house.'

But Brian held out. They would be gone by the time the teas started and meanwhile they were going to have the benefit of early morning light. The dogs and cat staked their claims next and on sunny days could be found luxuriating in the oblongs of warmth on the carpet. They brought their bones in to add a touch of interest at ground level and in no time the conservatory became just another living room.

Towards the end of February the weather turned foul; wet and so windy it shook the flimsy bungalow and blew away some panes of glass in the big greenhouse. The builders had finished the roof and gone which was a pity as they missed the satisfaction of seeing the results of their efforts – dry ceilings. At first we were sceptical but as the days passed with no leaks we relaxed and put the drip-catching buckets away.

We told everyone we had dry beds at last and persuaded some friends – Ian and Val – to come and stay for a few days. Like Brian they enjoy walking whatever the weather and on the second day of their visit the three of them cocooned themselves in rubber and prepared to go out. The dogs, not realising how hard it was raining, leapt about barking with excitement and Brian said he hadn't the heart to leave them behind. 'They can stay in the car if it's too wet for them,' he said, and off they all went. In the frenzy of finding gloves, scarves and leads, Honey's collar got overlooked, but when I found it in her basket I wasn't too bothered as they wouldn't be going on any roads.

Several hours later they returned, minus Honey. 'Is she here?' they said anxiously. 'Did she find her way home?' I shook my head and went to phone the police. The story of how they had lost Honey could wait, what mattered now was finding her. She was old and thin-coated, not the ideal combination for spending a night on Dartmoor.

While I was notifying the police and RSPCA, Ian, who is a great one for modern technology, issued each of us with one of his latest toys, a two-way radio handset and showed us how to use them, then we all went back to the place where they had last seen Honey and fanned out.

We walked and called until we were hoarse. Every so often the radio thing crackled and the four of us told each other where we were and where we were heading. It certainly saved going over the same ground twice. As well as his radio, Ian carried a cordless telephone which he had doctored in some way to make it possible to receive incoming calls. Now anyone phoning our home number would be able to speak to us direct. It seemed quite unreal to be stumbling across prehistoric Dartmoor waiting for an *incoming* call.

Darkness fell and we had to go home. In the morning I went out on Noah and asked every other rider I met to look out for Honey. Meanwhile, Brian, Val and Ian resumed the search on foot. It was late afternoon and we were all back indoors before the cordless phone rang (making me jump out of my skin) and a friend of mine said: 'Have you heard the news?'

'What news?'

'Prince Charles has got engaged. The girl's called Lady Diana Spencer, scarcely out of nappies they say. Anyway it'll help you to find Honey.'

'*Prince Charles* will help us to find Honey? Is he lending us his helicopter? What on earth are you talking about?'

'Faith, you're so dim. Phone your local radio station and

tell them about Honey. It's one of the few days in the year when people will actually be *listening* to their radios, not just leaving them on out of habit. Like the Iranian Embassy siege – when everyone was glued to their car radios – don't you remember?'

'OK, I'll try. Thanks for the suggestion, 'bye.'

I found the number of a local radio station and phoned them with the details of Honey's appearance and probable location. Then we detuned from Radio 4 and found the Devon wavelength. Sure enough someone was reciting Lady Diana's pedigree in between bouts of pop music that we had become so familiar with while the builders were with us. After one or two of these terrible records the presenter abandoned Lady Diana Spencer and asked listeners in the Dartmoor region to watch out for a small brown dog answering to the name of Honey. He gave our telephone number, then returned to the royal engagement.

Ian and Val had to return home before the end of the story. I daresay we could have phoned them in their car as they headed back to London but we didn't know how to, so we dialled their home number and left a message on the answering machine: Honey had been found.

She had trotted into a butcher's shop in a village some three miles from our home. The butcher, recognising her from the local radio description, had shut her in a shed before contacting us. Brian drove over to fetch her and was taken aback when she showed a marked reluctance to leave her new friend.

'You fickle old horror,' we told her, 'we've been worried sick about you.' She seemed none the worse for her ordeal. She disdained her meal, having already dined on best steak, and stretched out contentedly in front of the fire. We imagined she must have holed up somewhere on the moor overnight, then set out for home when it was light. Since we couldn't rely on Prince Charles to get engaged for our convenience again we bought a bell for Honey's collar and tried to make sure she always wore it when she went out.

Parsley and Ella were the only ones to benefit from Honey's adventure. Ever since Crufts on TV a week or so before, they had been suffering from my annual obedience training craze. A makeshift obstacle course in the sitting room was the centrepiece of their lessons which they endured rather than enjoyed. The last straw as far as they were concerned was having their bones used as training aids. They didn't in the least mind retrieving them but they objected strongly to dropping them at my feet. After the business with Honey I lost interest in their bones. Brian had a theory that they probably engineered the whole thing.

Chapter Eleven

IT SEEMED ODD hearing Brian on the phone ordering summery goods like hanging baskets and herbs. Outside, penguins would not have seemed out of place, the weather had turned so savage only two lorry drivers were able to deliver and parts of Devon were flooded. At first our own paddock was no more than spongy but inevitably it reached saturation point and springs began to bubble up here and there. Soon it was nearly all under a few inches of water. The ponies were disgruntled and huddled in their field shelter looking for all the world like drenched holidaymakers trying to keep dry in a bus shelter.

After several days of heavy rain we were woken one night by Noah whinnying and as he is not the sort to call for help unless it's urgent we went out with torches to see what was up. We found part of their roof blown down and both ponies soaking wet. We squelched through ankle-deep mud and led them out of their paddock to the relative dry of the garden. We looked at each other for ideas. What now? We had no proper stabling and their field was a pond.

'What about one of the greenhouses?' I said. As an opening bid it was weak.

'The *greenhouses*?' The way he carried on you'd have thought I was proposing to loose a herd of baboons in there, not two damply subdued ponies.

'A polytunnel then.'

'They'd rip it to pieces with their hooves.'

'Oh, for heaven's sake. They're hardly likely to lie on their backs waving their feet in the air. How about the conservatory?'

'I do believe you're serious.' He was off again, (now I was a candidate for Colney Hatch) ending with 'Why not bring them into the bedroom, it's got a nice soft carpet'. In the end though it was he who emptied the garden shed of tables and chairs and strawed it for them, an arduous job at three a.m. in teeming rain. In ordinary circumstances it would have been impossible to squeeze two fully grown ponies into a small shed but the circumstances were far from ordinary and in they went, backwards because there was more headroom by the door. Once in, they were wedged tight against each other with just enough room fore and aft for them to lower their heads to eat hay.

The next morning (or rather later the same morning) they were not what you'd call keen to leave their snug sardine tin and had to be threatened and bribed before they would come out. Looking at the size of them in daylight it seemed unbelievable that the whole mass of them had fit into the small shed – I remembered feeling the same sort of incredulity after Marcus was born – and hadn't panicked and kicked the sides down. Brian repaired their field shelter and we put them back with plenty of fresh straw to sop up the mud. 'It won't be for long,' we lied, having heard the forecast, and went indoors to phone my mother.

Anne's cottage was near the Dart, one of the many rivers currently bursting its banks and getting itself on the TV news. 'I'm *all right*,' she insisted, 'you don't have to keep phoning every five minutes to see if I've drowned.'

'Twice a day actually. I know you haven't drowned but have you done anything about your furniture yet? It said on the news that there's at least another twenty-four hours' rain to come.'

'I know. Eileen and Tracy' (her neighbours) 'have already taken up their carpets.'

'And have you? You'll have to leave the heavy furniture but you should be starting to clear your light stuff upstairs.'

'No, the river's miles away. It won't come in.'

'How far off is it exactly?' I hung on while she went to her French window. She came back and said there was a dead fish in the garden.

'A *fish*,' I howled.

'Poor thing. It looks like a salmon, it's got a nasty cut on its side.'

'Bugger the salmon – how far has the water risen?'

'Do stop shouting. The river is about five or six feet away from the house, I told you not to fuss. Do you think it would be safe to give the salmon to the cats if I boiled it thoroughly?'

I tore out what remained of my hair. 'Don't touch it, it might have been poisoned. Look, you've *got* to move your stuff upstairs. If the roads were passable we'd come over and do it ourselves but there are flood notices everywhere and we're stranded.'

'No, you mustn't risk going out in that leaky car of yours. Anyway, I shall stop the water coming into the house with the power of thought. I'll stop it going into Eileen and Tracy's house while I'm at it,' she added generously.

Brian, who had more faith in the power of sandbags than the power of thought, phoned Anne's local council, only to be told that they were doing all they could and that house-holders along the river should move upstairs.

During the next twenty-four hours the flooded Dart rose another three feet, causing Anne such annoyance that she rang an estate agent and put her house up for sale. 'It's practically floating,' she informed the agent. 'I'm not moving upstairs, I'd sooner move to a dry village.' Having put those wheels in motion she returned to her Canute act.

The flood water stopped just a few inches short of the glass in her French window. If there had not been a six-inch step below the frame no amount of thought power would have stopped it but as she said, that's splitting hairs. 'I kept next door dry too,' she said. 'I told them not to bother taking up their carpets.'

As soon as the roads were clear and delivery lorries able to get through again, preparations for the season ahead began in earnest. As before, all container-grown shrubs were labelled and put straight out on to the display beds while the dozens of boxes of bedding plants were taken into the propagation house for pricking out. Although pricking out was work we both enjoyed, we had slight twinges of panic when we realised there was no way two people could deal with thousands of seedlings in the time available. Young plants bolt into uneven growth if they are left too long in their nursery boxes; the ones on the outside are all right but the middle ones, competing for light, go yellow and leggy. We needed helpers. My mother came a few times but by now her attention was more on house-hunting and on being at home to prospective buyers. Any friend or acquaintance showing the slightest interest in botany was press-ganged into the greenhouse, issued with a dibber and set to work.

It wasn't a very satisfactory state of affairs since you can't expect untrained helpers to plant as uniformly as is required by a perfectionist like Brian. Then we had a stroke of luck. Some old friends with whom we had lost touch, a couple called Kevin and Denise, turned up out of the blue. After the small-world-isn't-it and fancy-us-all-moving-to-the-same-part-of-Devon sort of reunion they offered themselves as prickers out. 'We'll come in each day if you like,' said Denise. 'I know a bit about plants.'

She was being modest, she had a magical touch with plants, and Kevin, who started off hardly knowing a root from a shoot, was so quick to learn we were soon a pretty professional team. Each morning we would fill the liners (the plastic strips inside seed trays) with potting compost and stack them on the benches. When we thought we had done enough for a day's work we would start planting, twelve seedlings to a strip, four strips to a tray. Some, like lobelia or mesembryanthemum, were delicate and required a gentle touch so we tended to do those in the mornings when we were all fresh, leaving robust species for the end of the day when we were flagging. Young brassicas were particularly easy to transplant. They have fat, almost succulent first leaves which even a ham-fisted operator can grasp without damaging them. Out they would come, trailing their perfect little white roots, to be lowered carefully into the dibbed holes of the strip trays.

We had a lot of laughs too and were soon regarding customers as if they were gatecrashers at a party. What the customers thought about all the merriment in the greenhouse I can't imagine but it didn't keep them away.

One day Kevin and Denise roped in their two teenage daughters to help with the transplanting. The girls were exactly what a racehorse breeder would hope for if he put a French filly to an Irish stud; fine looks, good bone and kind temperament. They had stamina too, always a useful attribute in a horse or a horticultural worker. We were impressed and said we had not come across many teenagers willing to do a day's work. Denise who is French but speaks fluent English said: 'I can't understand it, they don't do a thing at home. You should see their bedrooms.' The girls groaned at this all too familiar refrain and said working in a greenhouse wasn't really *work* just a giggle.

To keep everyone fuelled or ill, depending on the outcome of the experiment, I had spent the previous evening making scones. My sanctuary friend Sylvia had advised me to buy McDougall's readymix as in her opinion it was the best, so for this prototype test I had made one batch of McDougall's, one of another brand and one with ordinary flour and fat. Now I carried the three sorts into the greenhouse and invited everyone to down tools and tuck in. 'There are three different sorts of jam too,' I told them. 'I'd like you to tell me which scone mix and which jam you like best. The cream is straight St Ivel, you needn't comment on that.'

The results of our consumer test would have sent the McDougall shareholders dancing in the streets. All six of us rated the McDougall scones way above the rest, perfect in texture and taste. My own, made with raw ingredients, came next although Kevin did say they would sink ducks and the other, a well-known brand, tasted of nothing much except bicarb and didn't score with any of us.

Hartley's jam beat Robinson's by a whisker – it had more recognisable lumps of strawberry in it – leaving the too sweet Co-op a non-starter. The cream of course was voted sheer bliss by everyone.

'Thanks everybody,' I said. 'I'll take the plates back and make us all a pot of tea to wash it down.' They staggered back to their benches looking a little the worse for wear after three scones and a mountain of cream apiece and I took the tray indoors well pleased with the test. Curiously enough I had never come across 'convenience' food before, always imagining that the sort of people who bought pre-prepared mixes must either be severely subnormal or convinced feminists. I was now more than willing to join their ranks. What a lot of time I could save – ready-mixed bacon and eggs, casseroles, curries, *salads*. No more washing earth off lettuces . . .

Back in the propagation house the finished trays of bedding stock were causing a bottleneck at the door. Four extra pairs of hands had made short work of petunias, marigolds, carnations and lobelia that day and there was still enough light left to make a start on some brassicas. Kevin and the girls wheeled the flower seedlings away to the cold greenhouse and Brian lifted a box of cabbage on to the bench.

'I hope we're going to sell all these,' I said, my mind still running on out-of-the-packet cooking.

'Why not?' said Brian. 'Who'd buy vegetables if they could grow their own?'

'I wasn't thinking of the growing part, more the cooking.' But Brian was telling Denise how well flavoured was the new F1 hybrid 'Minicole' cabbage. Plainly he wasn't yet ready to come with me into convenience catering.

It took nearly two weeks to prick out all the bedding and vegetable seedlings. Life outside the greenhouses must have gone on but we didn't see much beyond seed trays and compost. There was the budget – a particularly annoying one for the self-employed as petrol went up 20p a gallon – but other than that Martians could have landed and we wouldn't have noticed.

The cold greenhouse looked a picture when we had finished. Brian wanted to put the plants to harden off in alphabetical order from antirrhinum to zinnia but I was able to persuade him – with the aid of a pseudo-scientific article I had read – to try putting 'compatible' plants next to each other. (For the record, we found it didn't make the slightest difference to their progress even if two sworn enemies were laid next to each other. This is certainly *not* the case with cut

142

flowers as anyone who has tried mixing roses with daffodils will confirm.)

On the very day the last of the annual stock was finished a lorry came in with a delivery of dahlias and chrysanthemums. 'You said we'd *finished*,' I seethed.

'Only the annuals. Now we must start on the perennials. Look at that for quality – superb, aren't they?'

'Very healthy.'

'Do I sense a certain disinterest in these fine young plants?'

'Dislike actually.' He looked shocked so I amended it: 'Temporary dislike. I've *got* to have some time off to go to Exeter for the cream tea stuff. It'll be Easter soon and I haven't done a thing except paint the tables.'

'Of course you must go. Anyway there's no hurry to get this stuff potted, this afternoon would do.' He ducked as I hurled a flowerpot at him and caught it before it knocked something over. 'No, seriously, I'll see to the rest of the transplanting. You go off and enjoy yourself.'

Although I would never rate shopping as enjoyable I quite liked wheeling a trolley round the wholesaler's. Everything was larger than life: vast drums of oil for fish and chip shops, gallon-tins of vinegar, boxes containing twenty-four tins of this or that. I think the minimum order of some grocery items was twelve. I had my list with me and was determined not to be seduced into buying anything we didn't need but I weakened over a gigantic hotel-sized roll of cling film. It was so cheap, only a few pence more than the retail price of a small one and I'm still using it five years later. I also bought two seven-pound drums of jam, six catering-size bags of scone mix, sugar, a thousand best quality tea bags and a small drum of Gold Blend instant coffee. (Sylvia had told me to get coffee beans but I'm not very good at real coffee and challenge anyone to tell the difference if you make the Gold Blend hot and strong.)

After I had finished in the perishable section I hauled the trolley – as big as a bus – along to the hardware section. Here I deliberated for ages among a bewildering choice of china. It ranged from cheap and nasty to fine bone. Eventually I narrowed the field down to two possibilities – a blue and white traditional willow pattern or an elegant straight-sided brown cottagey design. With the weather still cold and blustery the temptation was to go for the comforting brown but I took a chance on having some summer and settled for the cooler blue and white. I asked the assistant for twenty cups, saucers and plates. 'Are you starting cream teas?' she asked.

'Yes, how did you guess?'

She smiled. 'I didn't have to guess the cream teas – you've got all the stuff in your trolley. I thought you must be a beginner though because you haven't allowed for breakages. Most of the old hands buy extra cups.'

'Oh of course. Thanks for reminding me, it's always cups, isn't it, that get dropped?'

'No, from what I hear everything gets dropped some time or other but it's only the cups that break. Are you taking on any staff?'

'No, it'll just be my husband and me.'

'Really? Your poor feet.'

I didn't like the sound of that. I knew my brain was going to ache from all the extra arithmetic but I hadn't bargained for mutinous feet as well. 'I've got a friend who used to do teas,' I said. 'She didn't say anything about feet.'

The assistant shrugged. 'People vary. My aunt does teas and she says what gets her down are the children. They make pigs of themselves on cream then they're sick.'

Suddenly I began to have Grave Doubts. Between Sylvia's Germans and this lady's aunt's vomiting infants the whole venture seemed unattractive, to say the least. 'I'd better go and choose some cutlery now,' I said lamely.

'Righto. I'll wrap your china for you while you have a look around. It's nice this willow pattern, isn't it? Don't you want any matching teapots and sugar bowls?'

'No, I've got masses of everything except cups, saucers and plates. We used to have a guest-house and I kept quite a lot of crockery.'

'A guest-house? I'd love that, specially in the evenings when the work's done and you can relax with the visitors.'

144

I left her to her illusions and went to choose some knives and spoons. Relax with the guests? Huh. It was more a matter of shouting up the stairs: 'If you're not in bed in five minutes you'll be for it' but then our guests had been mainly eight-year-old insomniacs.

Driving back through the countryside I was struck by how wintery everything was still. With Easter only three weeks away the only real indications of spring were banks of snowdrops, overhanging catkins and a few people cleaning up their B & B signs. Like a department store displaying jumpers in a heatwave, a business dealing in cultivated flowers and plants tends to give you a false impression of the seasons. For instance here, along the banks of the River Teign, clumps of daffodils were only at the leaf stage whereas in our sheltered bulb beds they were on the point of flowering.

'How was the wide world?' asked Brian when I got home.

'Backward. Not the wholesaler's, the scenery. People's gardens are still dark and drippy, hardly any colour. How is it that our iris crop has finished before it should have begun?'

'I heated the beds,' Brian said simply, 'and it was an early variety. It paid off, didn't it?' The cut iris had been very popular with the customers, probably they needed something cheerful what with the rain and the budget. One man had surprised us by buying fourteen pounds' worth all at once. Brian served him and when he had gone I said: 'That was quite a sale, Brian. Had he forgotten his wife's birthday or something?'

'His *wife*?' said Brian. 'Crikey, don't go putting your foot in it if his wife comes in, will you? Don't ask her how she liked the flowers.'

As soon as Garden Centre duties allowed, I baked and froze several hundred scones so as to have a stockpile when the time came. Mixing, rolling and cutting out took no time – they put emulsifiers in packeted mixes to make them idiot-proof – but I seldom saw eye to eye with the Rayburn when it was time to cook. I have always hated Agas and Rayburns. Their slow-wittedness compared to the instant response of gas stoves has often reduced me to physically abusing them and this one (which was already in the bungalow when we moved in) was no exception. It liked two hours' notice to get itself fit enough to tackle a couple of trays of scones and since Mr McDougall and I could prepare eighty in half an hour the waiting drove me up the wall. Aga and Rayburn-loving friends suggested pre-heating the monster at the beginning of the day so that it would be ready when I wanted it. That would have been fine if I had known for sure when I would be baking but often other jobs or customers prevented it and you have to be extremely wealthy to run a stove at 400°F for fun.

'I'm going to do the baking in the evenings in future,' I told Brian. 'I can't stand wasting daylight hours stuck indoors.'

'Oh,' said Brian cautiously. I could see him weighing up the pros and cons of this. Pro: She'll be able to serve the customers without worrying about the Rayburn blowing up. Con: She'll be kicking hell out of the Rayburn in the evenings instead of in the day; this will not be pleasant when I'm trying to read.

'But not yet,' I said. 'I've used up all the bags of scone mix. I'll make some more when half of these are sold.'

'How many have you made? Now, let's see what it all costs.' He took one of the empty bags and did some calculations on the side. 'It works out at 2½p per two-ounce scone.'

'I know.'

'*You* worked it out?'

'Sylvia told me it would come out at 2½p if I followed the instructions and even I can add gallons of water to heaps of flour. You should try it, it's as easy as mixing cement. Shall we work out the rest of the costs? There's jam and cream, tea, milk and sugar.'

Obviously the most expensive part of a cream tea is the clotted cream. This would cost £9.60 for a 6lb pack, maybe a bit less if I could find a farmer's wife selling it direct. Each customer would get a 2oz portion – about 16p. The rest of the food came to very little, not more than nine or ten pence.

'I won't add the cost of the tables and chairs and crockery,' said Brian. 'We can sell them off at the end of the season. So if you're lucky and don't drop too much you should make over fifty-five pence profit on each tea.' It wasn't a fortune but it was a satisfactory enough figure. Garden Centre customers fortified by a snack could well make a second circuit of the plants and if this happened the teas would have done a good job.

Marcus, now three months into his Indian travels, gleefully pointed out in his letters home that he could live for a day on the equivalent cost of one cream tea. He and his friend had landed at Bombay, travelled by train and bus ('lunatic drivers') to Goa, then on to Kerala in the south west. His letters were long and as interesting, to us, as Alistair Cooke's. He told of blistering heat, breathtaking scenery, poverty, political corruption and, most of all, *prices*. All his letters started like a shopping list, for instance: 'Best bananas only 5p a pound, they have thin skins and wonderful pink flesh and grow all over the place. Large brown loaf 3p, massive papayas 13p, soyabean mix 6½p for a large portion. Even *The Times* is only 3p.' He assured us over and over again that he was washing all his fruit and vegetables: 'I have been struggling to clean our fruit as scrubbing brushes seem to be unheard of here. Then we came across a little shop that had them in bristle so I bought a big one for 1½ rupees. At the same time I had a haircut in the street. A barber with five staff took measurements and instructions from me – I might have been the first ever white to set foot there. They all discussed the length and shape of the proposed crop, then I got a spray, a cut, shave, another spray and a blow-dry and the bloke was *still* fussing around with various implements when I eventually freed myself and paid. It was four rupees and a good haircut too.' He did his clothes washing in a bucket with a bar of yellow unscented soap (one rupee). The water (free) heated itself up in the sun. When the clothes were rinsed he laid them out on bushes and they were dry in twenty minutes.

It was not quite like that in Devon. The Easter weather was so cold and wet we postponed the teas for a further week. Nobody in their right mind was going to linger in a Garden Centre where high winds had ripped an end off one of the polytunnels and lifted eight boxes of perennial herbs off their bench.

'I think I'd like a nervous breakdown,' I said when Brian asked me what I would like for my birthday.

'Not in April you can't, there isn't time. Have you seen my two-inch nails anywhere?'

'You finished them when you mended the tunnel. I'll get you some more when I go out – I promised to take some peat to that woman without a car.'

I delivered the peat and drove back across the moor so that the dogs could have a run. It was raining too hard for them to want to stay out long so we all got back into the van. Then my attention was caught by a group of ponies huddling miserably together with their backs to the wind. Something looked wrong, they were standing too still. As I walked towards them all but three ambled stiffly away. Two of the remaining ones eyed me suspiciously but the third, the thinnest pony I have ever seen, just stood gazing apathetically into space. He was evidently very ill indeed, so cold he had lost the ability to shiver and so thin his ribs and spine were clearly outlined under his coat. I examined his gums and eyelids and tried to find his pulse.

There was a phone box back along the way I had driven and with a none too steady finger I dialled the RSPCA emergency number. An answering machine started its tape so I disconnected and dialled Sylvia's sanctuary. 'An emergency, Sylvia. I can't raise the R.S. Can you help?'

Sylvia's opinion of the RSPCA was short and unrepeatable. 'What's happened and where are you?' she said.

'A moorland pony, a four-year-old male. He's in a bad way. There's hardly a pulse. No colour in his mouth or eyes.'

'Sounds like a no-hoper. Tell me precisely where he is and we'll be there with a vet in half an hour.'

I gave directions and added: 'Could you bring some hay? There are some other very weak ones as well.'

The pony was exactly as I had left him, head bowed nearly to his feet. I tried to shield him from the worst of the wind but it was impossible. After about ten minutes his legs buckled and he crumpled to the ground. I put my anorak over his neck and held his head in my lap, stroking him and willing him to die quickly. But death from starvation is never quick.

For what seemed a long time, but was only fifteen minutes or so, the pony lay fighting for breath. He was bleeding internally now and blood came out of his mouth to be washed away by the rain. Then there were people – Sylvia and three or four sanctuary helpers and the vet who quickly examined the pony and shot him through the head without delay.

Someone took photographs, then produced a razor-blade and cut off one of the pony's ears. The pitiful corpse now looked grotesque. 'It's got to be done,' Sylvia said gently. 'It's the only permanent proof of ownership, in this case, the ear mark.'

'You don't seem at all surprised by this, Sylvia. I can hardly believe it's happening – animals starving to death in England.'

'Oh, it's happening all right. April is one of the worst months for outwintered stock; they've used up all their fat supplies and there's nothing for them to eat on the moor. Sheep, ponies, cattle, it's the same story for all of them.'

'But their owners— ' I began.

'Look, there isn't time now to go into the grisly facts. Go home and get yourself dried out. I'll ring you later.' And she was gone, sloshing through the mud to take hay to the group of shivering ponies, most of which would end up on continental dinner plates as soon as they were fat enough.

As a result of this incident I joined a charity called the Dartmoor Livestock Protection Society, a separate one from Sylvia's although the two work closely together. As the name implies, it protects moorland animals – a job which should be the responsibility of the moorland farmers – and enjoys the co-operation and support of the police, vets and RSPCA. The work is not unlike that of lifeboatmen in that volunteer members are on call twenty-four hours a day to go to the assistance of distressed or injured livestock – ponies, sheep and cattle. Sheep are especially at risk but there is virtually no shepherding on Dartmoor although thousands are grazed on open moorland throughout the year. A professional shepherd from the Peak District once told me he had never seen stock in such poor condition (this was in mid-summer) and that he would be ashamed if they were his. It's a pity that very few Dartmoor farmers feel this way.

Chapter Twelve

IT WAS WELL into the Easter holidays before we could begin to serve teas outdoors. Theoretically, we could have started off in the conservatory but by then we had made it so much an extension of our living room we didn't want strangers in it. 'It'll be Christmas if you don't get going soon,' Brian kept saying, so one morning, when it wasn't raining, I donned my dog-clipping overall (washed and ironed for the occasion) and hung out the two signs: Coffee and Cream Teas.

Shortly after nine thirty, when you would have thought holidaymakers would still be at breakfast, an American couple drove in and sat down at one of the tables on the lawn. 'Good morning,' I said, feeling rather as though I was acting a part. It was peculiar being scrubbed up like a surgeon first thing in the morning. 'Going to be a nice day, isn't it?'

'Is it?' said the man in surprise.

'She means the mercury hasn't hit zero,' said his wife with a smile and turning to me she said: 'A pot of coffee and sump'n to eat.' She had a soft drawly sort of accent which made the absence of 'please' somehow acceptable. (I later discovered that few Americans say 'please'; they don't mean anything by it, it's just their way.) But the 'sump'n to eat' threw me into a panic – I had completely overlooked the possibility of *morning* snacks. I went indoors and put the kettle on for their coffee. While it was boiling I slipped out of the back door and ran across to the greenhouse. 'Hey, Brian,' I whispered, 'here a minute.'

'Have you got a salesman?' he said sympathetically.

'No, it's a coffee couple. Americans.'

'At nine thirty? Can't they sleep?'

'Shut up. The coffee's no problem but they want something to eat and I haven't got anything special.'

'Give them a couple of bananas,' he suggested. 'They're quite nice with coffee. Filling.'

'I'm not starting a flaming greengrocer's. Would you pop down to the village shop for me and get some fancy biscuits? I'll stall them.' I went back to the kitchen and was confronted by problem number two. The woman had asked for a *pot* of coffee, not two cups. The price of a cup of coffee was 20p; the pot, if filled right up, held six cups. 'Oh hell,' I snarled and aimed a kick at my favourite enemy the Rayburn.

'Sorry to keep you waiting.' I limped over the grass to their table and put the tray down.

'Mm, smells good,' said the man. It looked good too in a dark brown coffee pot made at Honiton Potteries with matching cream jug and sugar bowl. I had also put a few stale digestive biscuits in a rustic little basket.

Arranging the cups and saucers for them I muttered 'That'll be fifty pence, please' and wished I could stop feeling so nervous.

'Thanks,' said the man and handed me 50p. I couldn't tell from his face if 50p seemed to him too little or too much for coffee and stale biscuits. 'Would you like cushions to sit on?' I said. 'Those chairs are awfully damp.' They said they would and when I fetched them a couple they became quite chatty and told me they had motored overnight from Norfolk. I said that was a long hop and the man said not if you come from Delaware it isn't. Equipped with only O-level geography I had to admit I didn't know Delaware from Tupperware so they drew me a map on the dew-covered table with their fingers. By the time Brian came home with biscuits from the village shop they had eaten all the horrible digestives and were ready to go.

'I don't think you're going to put Forte out of business,' Brian said, rather miffed at his wasted drive to the village.

'I'm sorry. I made a complete hash of that, didn't I? If a simple order like coffee and biscuits is going to send me into a flap I think we'd better scrub teas.' We looked at the 50p piece, conspicuously lonely in a new cash box, and suddenly saw the funny side. 'Fifty pence,' I giggled.

'Half a gallon of petrol, hot water, a basket of biscuits . . .'

151

'All for fifty pence and learning where Delaware is,' I finished. Then more cars began to trickle in so we both sprang back to our posts.

After that the morning went like clockwork. All customers were caught in one or other of our nets. Even the ones who started off 'just looking' found themselves looking over the rim of a coffee cup and paying 20p for the privilege. As we had anticipated, most of the garden enthusiasts took a second stroll round the display beds once they had had a half-time sit, and most of the people who came in primarily for coffee ended up in Brian's domain afterwards.

As the days passed I began to see a pattern in some of the holidaymakers' routine. Having had a large breakfast at their hotel or whatever, they would skip lunch so as to leave room for a cream tea in the early afternoon. Then they would burn it off with a strenuous walk or in some cases a strenuous drive and work up an appetite for dinner.

Another pattern which always amused us was what we called bonus customers. A car would be cruising along the road when one of the occupants would spot our refreshment signs and the car would jerk to a halt. Sometimes we would hear voices raised: Him: 'I don't want to stop here, it's only three miles to the next village.' Her: 'You never bloody well want to stop. We only saw Stonehenge because we needed petrol.' Cars would form a queue behind the arguers and *their* occupants would start: 'Oh, look at those lovely plants – shall we go in?' Or: 'I can sit in a traffic jam at home, let's get a cup of tea here.' All music to our ears and especially sweet when the first car drove blithely away leaving these secondary growths trooping in to spend money with us.

Providing we took lunch on the wing we soon found we could manage the two sides of the business fairly smoothly. If the Easter holidays had been sunny and warm it might have been a different story but the constant cold meant we could rush about without getting too tired and it kept the customers moving too. The growth of grass in the two large lawned areas was slow, which suited us as it didn't need much mowing. The weather also meant that birds nested late. When Brian went to repair part of a polytunnel one day he found a pheasant with a brood of chicks under one of the benches. She was very frightened so he postponed the repair job and took her some grain instead. I painted DO NOT DISTURB on a piece of wood and hung it on the door so that nobody would blunder in. She repaid us by bringing her chicks quite near the house each evening and letting us feed them. Small would have liked one of these fluffy morsels for supper but had too much respect for their mother's beak and watched from a distance.

Magnus, the dim-witted magpie, took a leaf out of Prince Charles's book and got himself engaged. We called his girlfriend Mrs Magnus but we were pretty sure their relationship was platonic. One of their problems was that she didn't like his friends. Magpies, in her view, ought to live in trees with other magpies, not perched on the backs of huge hairy creatures with hard hooves. But Magnus was loyal to Noah and Rory and wasn't going to give up a good billet to satisfy the whim of a mere fiancée. Each evening he would go to roost in their field shelter leaving poor Mrs M squawking with annoyance in the woods beyond the paddock. By day they pecked around together but it was a lukewarm relationship; the only interest they had in common was a liking for the scone crumbs customers left on the lawn.

It was early May before Devon saw the last frost and Brian was able to bring his geraniums and chrysanthemums into the open. The beds looked good, greened with the new season's stock. And in the polytunnel (not the pheasant's house) the display was as spectacular as it had been the previous year with massed non-stop begonias, fuchsias and hanging baskets. Out came the camera for the umpteenth time; sometimes I wonder if our descendants are going to think their ancestors *were* plants or puppies.

Dahlias were another line Brian grew, more for interest than profit, as many people don't like them. We potted them up in nine-inch polythene containers – the cheapness of these compared with hard pots enables the grower to hold the price down – and they grew like Jack's beanstalk, huge plants which attracted a lot of admiration and very few buyers. Dahlias house earwigs, there's no denying it, but we did get very tired of hearing this from the customers. I have rather a soft spot for earwigs; I don't know if it's true but I read somewhere that they are conscientious mothers. Judging by the health of the dahlias they seem to be conscientious tenants too; we couldn't see any evidence of them harming their hosts.

Cup Final day saw a predominantly female afternoon trade. This was a great improvement on the day of the Grand National when the only customers had been a middle-aged couple in the process of divorce. (If only people knew the acoustic properties of a polytunnel. This couple having settled on who was to have the carpets and the children were now bickering over the custody of their cat.) Our Cup Final grass widows had quite a spending spree, notching up over a hundred pounds in two hours, mainly on bedding plants which they said their husbands could plant after the match.

One evening when we were least expecting it the TV weatherman announced an area of high pressure.

'Does he mean us?' I called from the kitchen. Brian turned the volume up and I shot into the sitting room. Mesmerised we stared at our bit of Devon on the weather map. Prolonged sunshine, high temperatures? 'It is us,' Brian said, 'look at that section coming in from the west.'

'No clouds. I'd better make a double batch of scones.'

'And I'll re-pot the camellias. They might even bloom if they see some sunshine. On the other hand, they might die of shock.' He switched the television off and took his after-dinner cup of tea to the prop house. I made two hundred scones (I was getting quite good at it by now although I didn't like having to work in the evenings) and phoned a cream supplier to see if she had enough to see me through a possible upsurge of trade the following day.

'I'm sorry, my dear,' she said, 'you're too late. Some of my other customers heard the forecast earlier and all my cream is booked. Try St Ivel in the morning.'

That was the trouble with something as perishable as cream. You have to follow every single weather bulletin, then estimate the number of teas you expect to serve. Good quality cream has a fridge life of about three days – less if it's thundery – and although you can freeze it, it sometimes goes gritty in the process. Up until then I had been going to the St Ivel wholesaler twice a week – a round trip of an hour – and buying extra from a local Jersey herdswoman if I ran low. So far supply and demand had stayed the same but we were in for a surprise.

The next day there was a lovely blue haze over the countryside at dawn. By mid-morning we were so rushed off our feet with customers queuing for plants and coffee there wasn't time to go to the cream wholesaler's. Everything went swimmingly; the school holidays were over so nobody trailed cross children after them and nobody asked for the lavatory. After a brief lull for lunch it all started again. Tea for two, for seven, for four. I served, cleared, washed up, decanted more of everything into bowls and jugs, wiped tables, served again. One family admired the pot of flowering begonias decorating their table so I sold it to them. Brian came into the kitchen in some confusion. 'Do stop selling plants with the teas. I didn't know they'd already paid for it when I saw them getting into their car. Anyway they could have bought one off me.'

'They might have gone off the boil by the time they got to you. I thought it was clever salesmanship on my part.'

'Oh, all right. But put "paid" on any more you sell. By the way the dogs are scrounging again.'

'I'll get them. It seems a shame to keep them in on such a gorgeous day.' I went outside and hauled the dogs away from some customers who were giving them pieces of scone and jam. It was impossible to stop people feeding them, very few could resist three pairs of imploring brown eyes. I put them in the sitting room then the phone rang and a chirpy London voice said: 'Do you take parties?'

'What sort of parties?' I said, imagining a banner-waving political gathering.

'I'm a mystery tour today. Got twenty-two Ancient Britons on board. Nice old girls they are in the main – they want a cream tea.'

'Wheel them in,' I said enthusiastically and after ringing off rushed to the freezer to get forty-four extra scones (my maths

155

was improving) into the oven before they arrived. Half an hour later in they came, a party of OAPs from Bermondsey in London. They were accompanied by a handsome young Jamaican driver whom they called Black Beauty, presumably in retaliation for the Ancient Briton tag. 'Lovely, isn't he?' said one, giving him a cuddle as he helped her out of the minibus. 'Not a very fast driver mind, are you, luv?'

Beauty laughed and said he'd have got on a lot faster if he hadn't had to stop at every toilet for them.

'Better than the alternative,' someone called and this raised a chuckle all round. When the last lady had climbed stiffly from the bus I showed them across the lawn to the tea tables. There was a ripple of approval as they all took in the scenery.

'Smashing day to sit out. Look at all them sheep over on that hill.'

'Lovely. I like to see a few sheep.'

'I'd sooner have acrilan for the washing machine. Ooh, me feet – I must remember to sit on the shady side of the bus going back.'

'Are they conkers under that tree?'

'Fir cones, I think.' And to me: 'Are they fir cones, love?'

'Yes. They dropped off last year and we left some to see if they'd root themselves. They didn't, as you can see. Are you ready for your tea now or would you like to look round for a while?'

'Tea please.' They were unanimous.

Beauty followed me into the kitchen. I gave him a fiver which was the going rate for coach drivers who bring you extra trade. 'You've got a lively crowd, haven't you?' I said. 'I bet they keep you on your toes.'

'Great old girls, aren't they? And *talk* – blimey they never stop.'

'Perhaps they're afraid you'll fall asleep at the wheel if they don't keep you entertained. Give me a hand with these trays, would you? Scones and things first, then we'll come back for the tea. Tell me about this mystery tour.'

We ferried the trays to and fro. 'It's not a mystery any more,' he said looking crestfallen. 'They nicked my list when I was getting petrol, the old devils.'

156

'Oh, what a shame. Where were you planning to take them?'

'Well, the main place was going to be a cave of bats. I was really looking forward to that. I've never seen a bat. But someone said you wouldn't get her into a cave of bleeding bats if you bleeding paid her.'

'You got the impression she wasn't keen on bats?'

He grinned and nodded. 'Anyway that started the others off. They all started finding fault with the other places I'd ticked on my list. There was a salmon leap – I know it's the wrong time of year to see salmon jumping but I wanted to see the waterfall.'

'And they didn't?'

'No. I forget why. So then there was this butterfly farm.' We had been handing round plates as we talked and one of the old ladies called to the others: 'He's still on about those bloody butterflies.'

'Lay off him,' said another, drowsy in the sun. 'It's his holiday as much as ours.'

'It said in the brochure they were *loose*,' persisted the first. 'Filthy dirty things weeing all over our heads.'

The driver roared with laughter: 'How much wee could a butterfly do, Ma?'

'It depends how much it drinks,' said Ma logically.

'It's a bloomin' good job that cows don't fly' quoted the driver. This brought the house down. Brian, hearing their shrieks of laughter felt he was missing out and as his customers were quite happy to be left to their browsing he joined the tea party. They pulled his leg about his brightly coloured shirt, pretending to be dazzled by it ('It'll probably calm down with a bit of bleach') and tucked into their scones and cream. Then, to Beauty's dismay, asked for their teapots to be refilled.

'I'm taking them for a drive across the moor after this,' he said to me. 'It's going to be awful if I have to stop at every bush. I'll never get them back to their hotel in time for dinner.'

I sympathised but pointed out that it wasn't my job to ration people's tea.

'Anyway,' I said, 'there are loos at all the popular tourist stops.'

'Tourist spots? You wouldn't call Dartmoor Prison a tourist spot.'

'No, but you needn't go as far as the prison. The scenery is much prettier this side of the moor. In fact if you stick to the lower slopes you might even see some deer— '

'Sorry, I should have explained. It's *their* idea to go to the prison. They, er, they *insist* on it, you might say.'

'How morbid. It's a gloomy old dump.'

'It may be to you and me but some of them said it would be a journey down memory lane.'

'You're kidding – you don't mean— ?'

He nodded. 'I don't think any of them have got relatives inside at the moment – it's hard to tell who's boasting and who's not – but one or two said they used to visit there and they want to go again for old times' sake. It takes all sorts, doesn't it?'

'It certainly does. I wouldn't have thought anyone would want to look at a prison for sentimental reasons. You don't think they're planning to spring a prisoner, do you?'

'I wouldn't put it past them. Anyway I must go and round them up now. Thanks for the tea and scones, I enjoyed that.'

Watching him trying to assemble his flock I was reminded strongly of the difficulties Brian and I used to have with our guest-house children.* They too used to vanish when it was time to put them in the bus. Some of the old ladies were exploring the Garden Centre while others had disappeared into the greenhouses. One was having trouble with her shoes. 'Give us a hand, Beauty,' she called. 'I've drunk so much tea me shoes won't go back on.'

'Where's the lav, luv?' asked another.

At last they were in the coach with an exhausted Beauty mopping his forehead as he closed the doors. As a parting shot one of them tapped on the glass and shouted through the ventilator: 'Bet you didn't know your old man was running a

* The reader who would like to be reminded should turn to Faith's first two books – *The Year of the Cornflake* and *Green Behind the Ears*.

sex shop, did you?' but before I could make head or tail of this the coach moved off – destination H.M. Prison.

Within seconds of its departure a second coach drew up with a hiss of brakes and the driver, a young woman this time, called: 'I didn't know you took coaches. OK if we come in?'

Oh *no*, I groaned under my breath while at the same time trying to force a welcoming smile. 'It's not really convenient,' I said hesitantly. It seemed potty to turn away customers but I had by no means recovered from the last lot.

'We're only a party of twenty,' said the driver.

'But I haven't washed up yet. You saw that other coach leaving? Well they all had a cream tea and I haven't any more crockery until I've washed up.'

'Oh, if *that's* all,' said a brisk voice beside the driver. 'We'll wash up for you.' And to my astonishment they hopped out of the coach and streamed across the lawn.

It was like a dream. These pensioners, a lot younger than Beauty's – some a mere sixty-plus – swept aside my half-hearted protests and rolled up their sleeves. First they stacked the dirty crockery on to trays, then in single file they proceeded towards the kitchen. Their goodwill and kindness was almost overwhelming. 'You do look tired, dear. Show us where you keep the tea towels and leave the rest to us.' The six men in the party were issued with dish cloths and sent off to wipe down the tables. Someone heard the dogs whining in the sitting room and let them out. Brian came in to tell me the dogs were out again and he too was immediately engulfed in a wave of kindness. 'Sit down dear, you're all hot and bothered.'

'But my customers— ' Brian began (he said later he truly thought he must have flipped when he heard a total stranger inviting him to sit down in his own home).

'What's your name?' asked the head washer-up.

'Brian.'

'Well, Brian, would you like me to ask Harry to help you?'

'Who's Harry?'

'He's my husband. He's wiping the tables at the moment.'

'They're all helping,' I explained. 'I was caught on the hop

159

with nothing prepared so they offered to wash up. Divine intervention.'

'Oh.' He still looked baffled. 'I must get back.'

'We'll bring you a cup of tea,' said Harry's wife. 'Do you take sugar?'

'Yes, two please. But really you mustn't do all this . . .' He found himself gently shooed out of the door.

To my indescribable disappointment there was not enough cream left in the fridge to go round.

'I'm so sorry,' I kept saying. 'So sorry. If only your driver had given us half a day's notice . . . the other coach party, you see, they didn't book either.'

'Don't worry.' These wonderful ladies were not going to let me get upset. 'We'll make do with what there is.'

I was allowed to assist with the tea preparations. They divided the remaining scones and cream into half portions and re-set the tables. By now Harry and the other husbands had taken off their shirts and were sunbathing on the grass. I was instructed to wake them up and 'make them decent' before they had their tea. I found their bare torsos perfectly decent, not to say fanciable, but I did as I was told. Harry was very nice and didn't seem to mind his wife wasting her holiday in our kitchen. 'Dot can't settle to a holiday,' he said. 'She's never happier than when she's being useful. Same goes for the others, eh Mac?'

Mac said his wife loved housework. I was profoundly grateful to Brian's customers for keeping him out of earshot of this subversive conversation.

While the good Samaritans were enjoying their belated tea I took Brian a cup and found him persuading the coach driver to spend her five-pound tip on bedding plants. She was only too pleased to do so and said one of the perks of the driving job was having a huge luggage compartment. 'I bought some second-hand chairs on one outing,' she said. 'Normally I couldn't have got them home but with the coach I can drop things off at my house before I take it back to the depot.' She bought masses of bedding plants and when Brian wheeled the trolley to the coach the tea party called out: 'Leave some room for us, we're coming over for plants later.'

They were like the nicest possible aunts and uncles. By some oversight in my grandparents' breeding programmes I haven't any of my own but if I had I would have liked them to be like our unforgettable second sitting. We took photographs of them, well those who stayed still long enough. For no sooner had they finished tea than they were back on kitchen fatigues. They cleared, wiped tables, washed up, wiped up and then, because it was obviously the last catering session of the day (not a crumb of food left), they springcleaned the kitchen. A row of freshly washed tea towels fluttered on the line in the back garden. The kitchen itself was left as gleaming as it had been on the day the health inspector called. The only discordant note was struck when Harry pulled out his wallet and asked for the bill.

'Oh, I *couldn't*,' I said. 'Not after all your work. We should be paying you.'

He was adamant and I was adamant. In the end Brian sorted it out. 'You can have any plants at half price,' he said.

This went down well and there was a rush to choose plants. Brian wrapped and Harry stacked and the driver said the coach's axles would never take it. Then the cheerful party left, waving until the coach had turned the corner.

'What a day,' Brian said, 'and what lovely people.'

'What about the first lot, the Cockney grannies? They were amazing too. That reminds me, someone said you were running a sex shop. I wish you'd told me we're expanding.'

'Gosh, that old chestnut. She got the giggles over Pinus Contorta.'

'Oh how unoriginal.' Pinus Contorta or contorted Pinus was so frequently and deliberately mispronounced we had grown tired of the joke. 'Do you think this coach business is going to be a regular thing?'

'Maybe. That last driver said she would give us a day's notice in future so I'm sure she'll come again. She's very keen on gardening. Did you see the number of non-stops she bought?'

'I saw them in the luggage compartment. Come on, I'll give you a hand to re-stock the beds. You won't believe this but I've got nothing to do in the kitchen.' We tidied up the beds and had an argument about who was going to fetch fresh cream the following morning. We were both keen to go, not because the dairy held any magic for us but because whoever went would be spared an hour or so of our most unfavourite travelling salesman, Liam the Superbore.

We frequently had salesmen, or reps as they prefer to be called, and mostly they came, sold, had a cup of tea and went away again. But not Liam; he never sold us anything, never even discussed his wares. He must have been a dead loss to his company because he had no interest in his job, only in himself. To say he was boring would be like saying Sebastian Coe can run.

Like most families we keep a black list of bores – the sort of people you tell you're just going out when you've only just come in – and Liam headed the list from the day we met him. He was a hypochondriac with Walter Mitty leanings, a hide like a rhinoceros and, unfortunately, he was just old enough to have served in the war. Hearing him droning on about Dunkirk and Tobruk and the Rhine one almost wished the Panzer divisions been more successful in their single-minded pursuit of him . . .

In spite of his having, apparently, been everywhere, his grasp of geography was tenuous. One minute he would be staked out on the sand with Japanese ants chewing his face ('I expect you're wondering how I came by this scar?') and then with scarcely a comma he would be waist-deep in snow with only two dry matches between him and frostbite.

Addy only met him once but still dines out on it. She had been busying herself in the house while Brian and I were working outside. (This was before the cream teas started.) Enter Liam. We were in the habit of handing him over to each other when we had had enough, like the baton in a relay race. I took first stint and was treated to 'How I taught Peter O'Toole the art of making an after-dinner speech'. Brian, noble Brian, learned what it was like to live with half your bladder missing. With Liam a touch of prostate trouble easily became major surgery. Then it was my turn again. Drone drone drone, cricket this time – he had given the England selectors a few tips, prided himself, he did, on spotting promising young talent ... Brian was rescued from 'Did I ever tell you about the time I caught an art forger' by Addy calling us in for tea.

Brian and I sat down and seized books to read. Our incubus turned his attention to Addy, letting her into some culinary secrets hitherto known only to himself and the head chef at the Savoy. Addy retorted with some spirit that she had been browning beef like that before Liam was born and wouldn't his wife be expecting him home soon. Armour-plated Liam took his half bladder off to the loo.

'Why do you two put up with him?' said Addy crossly.

'We don't know how to get rid of him,' said Brian. 'We can't very well go out when he comes.'

'How often does he come?'

'About every six weeks.'

'Every six weeks? And does he always go on about his Boeuf Bourguignon? All that rubbish with the Savoy chef, who does he think he is?'

We sipped our tea in silence, glad of a few minutes' peace. The cistern flushed.

'Try and get rid of him, Brian,' Addy said as footsteps approached the door.

'Ssh, he'll hear you.'

'I'm not shushing' – the door opened – 'if you let him sit down again we'll find ourselves giving him breakfast.'

'Breakfast,' said Liam heartily. 'That reminds me of a breakfast I had to organise for the platoon in forty-four. We were cut off at the time and rations were low. My C.O. said to me, "Liam, my boy, if anyone can feed them you can." There were only a few eggs left you see and the cook— '

'No loaves or fishes?' Addy glared at him.

'No, dear lady, just a few eggs and a little flour. I cracked the eggs into a pan – a battered old aluminium pan it was – and I said to cook ...'

Brian and I exchanged glances and slipped out quietly leaving a bemused Addy pouring Liam his third cup of tea.

Chapter Thirteen

On the day Shergar won the Derby by ten lengths we were surprised to see quite a few customers waiting to be served. 'They'll have to wait,' I said. 'I've been looking forward to the race.' The theory about sporting events keeping people away was not infallible it seemed.

Brian, who is not interested in racing, said he would keep an eye on my side if I would get the trays ready. 'You've got ten minutes before the start,' he said. 'I'll go and take their orders while you set the trays.'

With one ear on the commentator reading the betting odds I hurriedly ladled out cream and jam into bowls and piled some warm scones on to baskets. Brian came in and made two pots of tea. 'They're Germans,' he said. 'A table of four and a table of five. Go on, off you go, I can manage.'

'That's why they're not indoors watching the race, I suppose. Thanks – see you in a minute.' I went into the sitting room and settled down to watch the runners being paraded. They were off. The going was good and Shergar ran the race of his life – the race that was to cost him his life – cantering home ten lengths clear.

'Fantastic,' I said to the dogs. They didn't think being shut in a darkened sitting room in the middle of the afternoon was fantastic at all. 'Come on, let's go and tell Brian.'

Brian, having served the nine teas, had returned to the shop where he could oversee both sides at once. 'I'm back,' I called.

'Good race?'

'Fantastic. The Aga Khan's Shergar – walked it. Teas OK?'

'Mm, all paid. No problems.'

I walked across to the tea customers to see if they wanted more hot water and was surprised to see that their pots of jam were empty. 'I'm so sorry,' I said, 'I thought I had filled them. I'll get you some more.' Puzzled, I returned to the kitchen. Surely I *had* filled them? Maybe I'd forgotten in my hurry to watch the Derby. I took two clean bowls and spooned half a pound of jam into each one.

'Here you are.' I put the jam on their tables. 'Can I get you some more hot water?'

'Thank you, Madam. This is a most wonderful tea.'

I smiled to myself as the kettle boiled. If I had served a Yorkshireman with the anaemic brew favoured by Continentals and Americans he wouldn't have called it wonderful. People's tastes varied so much, I had discovered. Broadly speaking, you could please everyone if you worked on the assumption that English people with northern accents liked strong tea, everyone else medium to strong, and foreigners coloured water.

I couldn't believe my eyes when I went back with the hot water. The second serving of jam had vanished. And the bowls of cream had hardly been touched. 'Don't you like cream?' I asked.

'Cream,' said a fattish woman. 'Ya, the cream is very nice but the fruit is wonderful. Some more if you please, Madam.' She held out the empty jam bowl. 'And what is the name you are calling it?'

'Hartley's strawberry jam,' I said trying not to laugh.

'Hartley's strawberry jam,' she repeated. 'I vill remember.'

For the third time I filled their bowls and for the third time they ate it all. Three pounds of jam between nine people. They ate it with their teaspoons and scraped the bowls clean. No wonder Sylvia had told me I would be in for a surprise when Germans came to tea. From the financial point of view I had made a huge profit because their virtually untouched cream could be chilled and recycled.

After this episode I paid more attention to the nationality of customers and noticed that nearly all Germans had a sweet tooth. The Dutch went for the cream, the French pecked messily at everything but seldom finished anything while the Italians, usually travelling with such extended families that one lot could seem like a package tour, went through the food like soldier ants. It was only the Germans who were prepared to pay 85p for a meal of jam.

One good thing about Continentals was that they didn't feed the dogs at the table. I know our dogs shouldn't have been at their tables but they were. For some weeks I tried keeping them in the kitchen but as the season grew busier it was too much trouble to shut the door with my foot when I was carrying trays so I let them loose. Most people liked dogs and some of my 'regulars' brought their own dogs out of their hot cars for a bowl of water. This didn't always go down too well with the other customers. 'Can't you *read*?' said one old killjoy to a family with a labrador. 'There's a notice at the entrance that says No Dogs.'

The family, a young couple with two babies and the labrador, settled themselves at a table and the husband said mildly, 'It says no male dogs and it only applies to the Garden Centre.'

The cross woman turned to me: 'It shouldn't be allowed, it's unhygienic. Dogs sniff things.'

'It's not unhygienic to sniff if you're a dog,' I said. 'It's the way they communicate.'

'I don't want to sit at a table that's been sniffed.' She glared at the labrador which hadn't done anything except sit placidly. 'I'm going to take my things to that furthest table.'

That furthest table was under a tree and also under the tree, as she soon discovered, were three more dogs – Honey, Parsley and Ella, taking their ease in the shade.

'This place is nothing but *dogs*. How ever did you get a licence?'

'I went to the post office,' I said, deliberately misunderstanding her.

'Not a dog licence, a *food* licence. I don't suppose you've got one of those either.'

'Oh yes, we jolly well have,' I said, needled by the implication of 'either'. 'The health inspector said my kitchen was— '

'It's like the streets of Cairo. Mangy things roaming the gutters. I shan't come here again, I can tell you.' She swept off to her car and drove away.

166

'Oh dear.' The young couple and I looked at each other like schoolchildren ticked off by the headmistress. 'That was our fault, wasn't it?' said the girl. 'Perhaps we shouldn't have brought Sam.'

'You bring Sam any time you want to,' I said. 'I'd much rather he came than that old battleaxe. Anyway it was our dogs that really wound her up.'

'Mangy things,' the girl giggled. 'Streets of Cairo . . . I say do you think we could have a cup of coffee, please? And a few biscuits for the children?'

'And don't sniff them,' the young man called after me as I went towards the house – 'It's unhygienic.'

Shortly after this our dog numbers increased still further. Parsley's puppy Shandy (né Snuff) came to stay for a fortnight while his owners went away on holiday. It was lovely to have him back. In some ways he looked younger, having lost the puzzled furrowed expression of the infant spaniel, but in other ways he was very much the teenager – clumsy, accident-prone and permanently hungry. He felt sleek and silky, his baby fluff gone and his coarser adult hair still to come. He was a most stable youngster – his owners had reared him to be well-mannered and friendly – and as obedient as could be expected in a half-grown dog.

At first Parsley was horrified to see him return to the nest. Her reaction in human terms was one of tight-lipped disapproval, not unlike that of a friend of ours who thought she'd launched her son safely into the world, then saw him coming up the path with five suitcases and his drum set. But half-way through the first day Parsley seemed to understand that the energetic little lodger had only come for a holiday and she stopped sulking.

With Shandy around the dogs didn't get much peace in the daytime. He wanted to play with them and in the end they usually gave in to him and went off to the woods at the back of the paddock. Here they could chase rabbits or squirrels and, on one occasion, a snake.

Ours was a part of Devon a little too abundant in snakes. One local customer told us she had had to move house because she was terrified of the number of adders which always came to sun themselves in her garden on hot days. 'They used to lie on the granite slabs,' she said, 'dozens of them. I could never sunbathe and sometimes there were so many I was afraid to hang the washing out. So I sold the house.'

'Didn't the new people mind snakes?' Brian asked.

'I don't know. I sold the house during the winter.'

But to return to the dogs' snake. It was an adder, quite a big one, and the dogs had injured it. Their barking brought us up to the paddock to investigate. Normally preferring to live and let live, on this occasion it seemed best to kill it rather than let it go away possibly in pain. Brian killed it with a spade and spoke sternly to the dogs about the dangers of fooling about with adders. We left it lying in the grass and went back to work.

Unknown to us, the dogs made their way back to the scene. A while later they appeared on the front lawn and in front of several tea customers proceeded to sick up bits of snake. It was awfully embarrassing – far worse than the streets of Cairo.

I shut them in a spare bedroom with newspaper on the floor while Brian dumped buckets of sand over the heaps on the lawn. The tea people didn't linger so when they had all gone I tracked down Small and gave her an emetic to be on the safe side. She brought up not snake but a whole mouse. Only a little one. It came out tail first and what amazed me was its pelt which had become detached at the head and now hung round its ankles making it look exactly like an undressed baby.

Sometimes I forget that not everyone shares my enthusiasm for pathology. (This started when, as a teenager, a medical student had smuggled me into the dissecting rooms of his hospital for a dare. The joke backfired on him because instead of fainting I showed keen clinical interest in the formalin-preserved bodies and asked if I could have a go with a scalpel.)

'Look, Brian,' I said holding out the mouse. 'Small sicked it up *whole* – look at the way the fur— '

'Push off.' His reaction was predictable enough.

'What have you got dear, a kitten?' asked an elderly woman who was choosing geraniums.

'No, a mouse. Our cat caught it.' I opened my hand to show her. She reeled as though she had received a right hook to the jaw and Brian had to fetch her a chair from the shop and fan her with a catalogue. 'You're bloody certifiable,' he whispered savagely and waved me away.

'Oops sorry.' I withdrew tactfully and put the mouse in the dustbin.

There was no getting away from it – neither of us was cut out to be a shopkeeper. Here we were, often with frayed tempers, trying to maintain a civilised front to the public, when what we really wanted to do was work without interruptions. There never seemed time to finish anything.

'How much longer is it all going to take, Brian?' I said after we had made our peace over the snake and mouse business. 'I hate it here.'

'So do I. I had Goddard in again this morning. I'll strangle him one of these days. Pass me the calendar . . . look, it's nearly July. Let's pull all the stops out and aim to put the place on the market in December. There's still a hell of a lot to be done.'

'I know. We must finish decorating inside the house, then paint the outside. The paddock needs attention too. How about the greenhouses?'

'They're not too bad. I've re-glazed the broken panes so all we need to do at the end of the season is clean and sterilise them.'

'I want to try to fit in some more dog clipping and I must find some time to revise my manuscript.'

'I think you'll have to shelve dog-clipping for a while. As for writing, couldn't you do it in the evenings?'

'Most evenings I'm baking scones.'

'OK. Cut out housework and write in the mornings. The coffee customers don't have to have your undivided attention.' It was a nice touch of diplomacy on his part to say 'cut out housework'. He must have noticed that deep litter

169

chickens would have felt at home in our living quarters.

Taking comfort in the fact that we were three-quarters through our two-year plan we doubled our vitamin B doses (if you take a megadose of B you don't need so much sleep) and headed for the finishing post. Brian rigged up a desk – a door balanced on two tea chests – in the shop so that I could write in there and keep one eye on the customers driving in. If they were Garden Centre customers I would ring a bell to attract Brian's attention and if they wanted coffee first I would go and see to them myself.

I think more chapters of *The Year of the Cornflake* than ever got into the book were used to wrap customers' begonias. For of course I was subtracting material all the time: those 125,000 words had to be reduced to 65,000 and the discarded pages ended up on the pile of wrapping paper we kept in the shop. At first I didn't like the cutting process but after a bit of practice I became Attila-like and wiped out whole families without a qualm. Animals had to be decimated too. As Wally said in one of his letters: 'No editor is going to put up with a brain-damaged rabbit with nine *named* babies for God's sake,' so poor Old Flopsy and Co had to go.

There were distractions. As I've said, the polytunnel (which was adjacent to the shop) amplified people's voices. There were hot-headed arguments; sympathetic sharing of troubles; affectionate, not to say passionate, declarations; and conversations on topics ranging from the recent shooting of the Pope to what's for dinner. One of my most treasured eavesdrops was an exchange between a party of prep-school boys and their young master. He was taking them to Exeter to a children's concert and their minibus had boiled over, so while he was waiting for it to cool down he brought the boys into the Garden Centre. They grumbled as boys will about being too hot/hungry/bored. 'Do we have to go to this fearful concert, sir? Can't we go swimming?'

'You'll enjoy it, Robin.'

'No I won't. The last one went on for ever.'

'Sir – why do they always have a slow movement in the middle of music? It's dead boring the slow movement.'

Perhaps Sir didn't know why they had a slow movement

but at any rate he did what any teacher with his wits about him would do and tossed the question back to the children. 'Why is there a slow movement, boys? Yes, Giles?'

'So's everybody can get their breath back, sir?'

Nature study was another distraction. A family of green woodpeckers, two newly-fledged youngsters with their parents, used to perch on some near-by telephone wires. Their forays into the woods for food and their subsequent regatherings were far more interesting than slaving over a mouldy manuscript. With some difficulty I disciplined myself to leave the binoculars indoors otherwise I might have been tempted to look even further afield. There were foxes and deer to be seen on distant hills if one had the time to sit and wait but time was a luxury we couldn't afford. There was also a badger in the vicinity, a lawn-digging night visitor which left unmistakable evidence of its presence but which despite a few dusk vigils we never even glimpsed. All we learned about badgers was that they liked bread, cheese, spaghetti bolognese and neatly mown lawns.

Wimbledon men's finals day dawned hot and sunny and we were rushed off our feet with morning customers. Everyone was talking about the match, the now historic Borg/McEnroe marathon, and everyone was rooting for Borg. The heat had an interesting effect on their choice of plants.

Brian, wheeling a trolleyful over from the cold frames for the fourth time that morning, called out: 'What's come over the customers today? They've gone blue.' His trolley was laden with predominantly blue or white shrubs or roses.

'It's the weather,' I said. 'Nobody wants red or oranges in this heat.'

'They've even gone off Peace and Superstar.'

'But that's terrific, we're getting low on those. What are they taking?'

'Blue Moon, would you believe? And Iceberg.' I could believe Iceberg, a beautiful floribunda, but Blue Moon was a different matter. A hybrid tea rose noted for its scent, its appearance in my opinion is quite off-putting. The colour isn't a true blue but cyanosed like the lips of a patient with breathing problems. So, although we didn't much like the hot sunshine ourselves we were very pleased indeed to have this unforeseen bonus of people buying things we normally found hard to shift. And for the first time I was glad I had chosen the willow-pattern cups and saucers.

At two o'clock we closed the Garden Centre, the first time we had done so since our day off for fishing, and settled down to enjoy Wimbledon. We both still remember the bliss of that half day off duty, the welcoming comfort of armchairs, the delicious guilt, and a match so enthralling we brought an electric kettle into the sitting room to make tea without having to miss a stroke. A great afternoon made even more enjoyable by seeing the loutish McEnroe beaten by a whisker.

Afterwards we took the dogs for a walk and came across a cool clearing in some woods with a river winding tidily through. It was simple and perfect and gave the impression of having been designed by a god in a good mood. Returning home we found a young couple sitting at one of the tables on the lawn. 'Hullo,' we said. 'Was there anything you wanted or are you just having a rest?'

The youngsters went red and the boy gulped and said sheepishly: 'Actually we were wondering if we could possibly . . . um, it's an awful cheek . . . please say if it's inconvenient . . .' He looked about fifteen.

'Spit it out, son,' Brian said. 'Have you run out of petrol?'

'Oh no, we walked,' the girl contributed. 'We've been walking on the moor and then we saw your cream tea sign . . .' She too tailed off in confusion.

'And we've never had a cream tea,' continued the boy. 'Never been to Devon actually. And it looked so lovely here we came in. We've been watching the sun go down.'

They were so young and so pretty we made them a slap-up tea and hoped they never guessed that we adjusted the price to suit their obviously limited means. After we had finished our own meal we glanced out of the window. They were still there, sitting on the grass now, holding hands. If there had been enough light I would have photographed them. They were as appealing as puppies.

'I wonder where they're staying tonight, Brian.'

'They're camping. Didn't you see their rucksacks? And in

answer to your next question no, they're *not* staying here.'

'Not in the paddock? There's plenty of room for a tent.'

'No.'

'But they're so sweet. They must be tired if they've been walking all day.'

Brian reminded me that teenagers are only ever tired when there's washing up to be done. 'I'll go and talk to them,' he said. 'You stay here.' He returned a moment later and picked up the car keys: 'I'm going to run them out to that clearing by the river we found today.'

'People aren't allowed to camp in the Park.' I followed him outside and said to Romeo and Juliet: 'If you get caught by a Ranger, come back here, we've got plenty of space for your tent.'

'Thanks very much. And thank you for the super meal,' said the boy. I resisted the temptation to rumple his curly locks, and waved them goodbye. Even if a Ranger did find them – unlikely in the secluded glen – he could hardly claim they were spoiling the scenery. Brian was right though, they didn't look at all tired.

One family which definitely did spoil the scenery were the peeing Italians. Sara and her friend Cathy were spending a short holiday with us and one morning before there were any customers about Brian asked them to move the sprinklers from the display beds to the tea lawn. 'Just freshen it up,' he said. 'Ten minutes either side will do, then put the sprinklers back on the Garden Centre.' He went off to work in a greenhouse and I settled down at the desk in the shop.

Sara and Cathy changed into bikinis before starting to drag the hose reels from A to B. When the two sprinklers were in place they turned on the taps and dared each other to run through the icy showers. They were having a riotous time when along the road came two cars, both crammed with people. I glanced up and called to the girls: 'If they come in for coffee you'd better turn the sprinklers off.'

'OK.'

I busied myself at the desk and didn't actually see the next move. The girls continued to shout and laugh then suddenly their laughter turned to outraged screams: 'Faith, look at those men! They're going to *pee* in our *lay-by*.'

I shot out of my chair. Three men had got out of one of the cars and were lining up against the Garden Centre wall unzipping their flies. 'Stop,' I shouted but they were looking, *ogling* at the girls and didn't hear me.

'Sara, they're Italians,' Cathy yelled. 'Your ex was Italian, wasn't he? What's the Italian for stop peeing?'

Sara, tears of laughter streaming down her face, said it was a phrase that had never cropped up in conversation with Luigi.

The men were now poised for action, three pink prawns at the ready. The girls leapt for the sprinklers, unclipped them, and with the full force of tap pressure applied their hoses to the men's hoses. 'Buzz offo,' commanded Sara. I clutched the shop door for support, helpless with laughter. Shocked into action the men moved along the wall where they thought they would be safe from attack but they had reckoned without our intrepid pair. With their reels spinning behind them the girls charged along the top of the wall spraying water accurately, first at the men's faces and then down below again. The occupants of the second car, wives and children, wound down their windows and yelled encouragement, in Italian, so it was hard to tell whose side they were on.

'Please,' gasped the eldest of the incontinent trio, 'toilet please.'

'No,' chorused Sara and Cathy. 'No toiletto.' The men, still unzipped, ran along the road heading for some woods beyond the car park. The distance was some fifty feet and as our hoses were a hundred feet they didn't stand a chance. 'Head them off, Cathy,' Sara yelled and sprinted after them. Cathy reached the path to the woods first and barred the way while Sara cut off their retreat. 'No, no,' screamed the wives as their menfolk were caught between two crossjets of hosefire. 'Too much wet.'

The men stopped. 'You are bad girls,' groaned one miserably. 'We are much wet.' They fastened their trousers and hurried back to the lay-by still pursued by the girls. Sara was chanting 'pronto pronto' and Cathy something I couldn't catch. Brian appeared and stopped open-mouthed at the sight of two carloads of jabbering Italians apparently being refused admission by our girls. 'Why are we turning customers away?' he asked. The detached academic way he said this was the last straw. I slid on to the grass and lay there half paralysed with laughter. 'Flashers,' I managed to croak.

'Faith, I realise it's a hot day but you can't seriously expect me to believe in flashers *plural*. There are nine or ten people in those cars. And why is Cathy sounding like a Latin text-book?' Without waiting for an answer he walked over to the taps and turned the water off. The Italians, still all jabbering at once, drove away.

'Hi Brian.' The girls waved triumphantly. Sara said: 'Wasn't Cathy good? She remembered her Latin O-level. She told them to go in Latin.'

'Actually, she told them to glow,' Brian corrected. '*Incandescere* doesn't mean go.'

'It's better than buzz offo,' said Sara loyally. 'That's all I could think of.' Brian's expression of total perplexity started us off again and it was some time before he was fully in the picture. He congratulated them on their quick thinking, then found them a job in the paddock, well away from the customers.

When they had dried their hair and changed we gave them each a polythene dustbin bag. 'Have you ever pulled ragwort, Cathy?' Sara asked. Cathy said no there wasn't a lot of ragwort in her Highgate flat and why did it need pulling anyway? Sara and I showed her the bright yellow weeds in the paddock. 'It's all poisonous,' I explained. 'Flowers, leaves, stem and root. Luckily it's shallow rooting so it pulls up easily. Animals wouldn't normally eat it but when it dies they might mistake it for hay and it's even more poisonous when it's dry. Put it in the bags and we can incinerate it later.'

Their help was invaluable. They cleared the paddock of ragwort, then topped the thistles and docks with billhooks, not an easy job with two ponies breathing down their necks and three dogs darting in and out of the long grass in search of imaginary foes. They enjoyed helping with the teas too until the very last day of their holiday when Sara received an insult.

It was actually meant as a compliment but Sara took it as an insult. She had carried a tray to the table where a party of six elderly women were sitting. 'Thank you, my dear,' said one and turning to me (I was clearing another table) asked 'Your daughter?'

'Yes.'

'Fine sturdy girl, isn't she?' said the woman admiringly. Oh God, I thought, please stop at sturdy, *please* don't say—

'Athletic,' said the woman, 'good at games, I don't doubt.'

My fine sturdy daughter, scarlet with rage, ran indoors and flung her shorts on the floor. 'I'm *never* showing my legs in public again,' she vowed. 'Never. It's jeans and maxi skirts from now on.'

'It was a *compliment*, Sara.' But the combined reassurance of Cathy, Brian and myself failed to convince her that she didn't look like a scrum-half. 'Sturdy,' she repeated gloomily at intervals, throughout the evening. Naturally I came in for most of the flak 'force-feeding us cod-liver oil when we were little' and so on.

Oddly enough, another customer at a later date made a similar sort of remark. A man and his wife were having tea at one table and a mother with two schoolgirl daughters at another. The girls, who were about fourteen and fifteen, wore the uniform of a local private school – gingham dresses, straw hats, leather sandals and white socks. They had clear complexions and a robust outdoor air about them. The man at the first table kept staring at them admiringly. 'Good-quality girls they are,' he said to his wife who immediately took offence and said 'Meaning our Jackie isn't, I suppose?'

'Jackie never sits up nice and straight like them.'

'Jackie don't go to private school.' She let the unspoken implication sink in before tossing the ball neatly into his court: 'And if you're so keen on people sitting up straight you can stop eating your dinner in front of the telly.'

Of all the cream-tea customers we liked the coachloads of pensioners best. It seems to me that once people have weathered the two decades from sixty to eighty they come to terms with chalky joints and dodgy bladders and take on a new zest for life. One group we had was very lively indeed. They lived in sheltered accommodation so presumably were too frail or too ill to cope independently but you would never have guessed. Their warden, a nice but slightly anxious young woman, tried to persuade some of them not to have a big tea as they had already had fish and chips for lunch. But the old ladies were in party mood and determined to enjoy every moment of their day out. They pooh-poohed the idea of indigestion tomorrow and ordered a cream tea for everybody. One, the star turn, ate three scones piled high with cream and earned herself a round of applause. 'It's my pacemaker,' she told me happily. 'I can eat what I like now I've got one.'

'A whole box of chocolates last week,' said her friend. 'Her nephew bought them for her, the one from Brighton.'

'But,' I said, avoiding looking at the warden who was rolling her eyes skyward, 'I didn't know pacemakers helped your digestion. I thought they were to help your heart.'

'Doctors don't tell you everything.'

'They haven't got time.'

'Take artificial hips. They go better on rich food too, don't they, Cissie?'

'She's a marvel, isn't she? You'd never think she was eighty-six.'

'Eighty-seven.'

'Cissie! I was at your eightieth. I can count, you know.'

'Ladies, ladies,' said the warden. 'Your tea's getting cold.'

'. . . that Emily over Plymouth way.'

'What about her?'

'Calling herself a white witch now.'

'Never.'

'She is. Honestly I've got more magic in my hot-water bottle than that stupid Emily's got in her whole body. I blame that local paper – fancy putting her picture on the front page. It's things like that get witches a bad name.'

I think it was about this time that British Rail started offering free transport to sick hedgehogs. It was on the ten o'clock TV news one evening. We were reading, not paying much attention to the screen which was showing the usual ration of peoples not managing to communicate with each other when suddenly the newsreader smiled and said something about hedgehogs. I parked my book and sat up. Brian carried on reading.

Because of the decline of the number of hedgehogs in Britain (said the newsreader) British Rail was pleased to announce a new service. Anyone finding an injured hedgehog could take it to the nearest railway station and have it sent free of charge to the hedgehog hospital in Buckinghamshire. There it would receive medical treatment and after convalescence would be re-homed in suitable surroundings.

Then the camera switched from the newsroom to the hedgehog hospital and we were shown a few of the patients, one of which was in splints. The item ended with a close-up shot of a polythene tray containing some healthy hedgehogs and on the side of the tray in big blue figures was a telephone number.

Thinking it would be nice if we could get hold of a breeding pair I copied down the number and when the news was over told Brian I was going to phone the hospital and get some more information. The gardener in him was all in favour of acquiring as many slug-eating little friends as possible but his pessimistic side foresaw all sorts of difficulties in getting them from Bucks to Devon. B.R. had not mentioned free *outbound* transport.

'It's worth a try,' I said. 'They'll probably get hundreds of phone calls offering good homes but if I phone now we could be among the first.'

I dialled the number. It rang and rang but there was no answer. Brian thought they must have all gone to bed but I couldn't imagine anyone with sick animals to look after going to bed at ten-thirty so I hung on and let it ring. I felt rather guilty in case my phone call was interrupting a tense moment. I pictured a nurse mopping the sweat from a small prickled brow while further down the ward a post-op patient was having his appetite tempted by a dish of finely minced snails. After about ten minutes I was just about to ring off when someone answered. 'Yes?' said a woman's voice. She sounded quite unfriendly so I apologised for phoning and said if it was inconvenient I would try again later.

'*Later*? I'd just managed to get off to sleep when the damn phone woke me. Who are you and what do you want?'

I was rather taken aback. Surely she must be used to strangers phoning? And who was seeing to the night feeds?

'I'm awfully sorry,' I said, 'but I thought as hedgehogs are nocturnal you'd be busy— '

'Hedgehogs? Did you say hedgehogs? Who the hell are you?'

'You don't know me,' I said, 'but I got your number from the TV news tonight. This is the hedgehog hospital, isn't it?'

There was an ominous silence for a moment then an emphatic, 'It certainly isn't. This is a private house.'

'But your number was shown on the news,' I persisted. 'I copied it very carefully as it was longish.' Then I started to tell her about the hedgehog rescue scheme but far from being interested she became crosser and crosser. She was appalled at the thought that mine mightn't be the only call and said she was going to ring up and complain to the BBC, then leave the phone off the hook. Before I could tell her it was *ITV* she wanted, she had rung off.

It must have been a batch number written on the side of the hedgehog tray, we decided, and it was a bit of bad luck that the woman who had it as a phone number wasn't a hedgehog enthusiast. But as we forgot to watch the news the following evening we never found out for sure. The next time we did watch, hedgehogs had made way for a crucial by-election.

Chapter Fourteen

THE WARRINGTON BY-ELECTION, normally the sort of event I find about as riveting as a dead slug or a pop record, was enlivened for us because one of our friends was standing as an independent candidate. Ian (of Ian and Val, the cordless-phone friends who had helped in the search for Honey) took a few days off work and roared north on his motor-bike to canvass votes. Looking at him on the television news was an odd sensation, like seeing some private possession put up for auction. 'He's wearing a *suit*,' I said in amazement. The phone rang: 'Ian's on the box,' said Sara, 'in a *suit*,' and rang off.

We watched the repeat on the later news and were amused to see that as well as the suit, Ian was wearing an almost invisible earpiece. 'He's listening to his radio,' Brian said jealously (he would have liked a sophisticated radio like Ian's). 'He's got a nerve, hasn't he?'

'Well, he wouldn't miss a concert for a by-election. He won't win, will he?'

'No, he's only doing it for fun.'

Roy Jenkins won the by-election but Ian didn't come away empty-handed. One of his supporters gave him a kitten which undoubtedly brought him much more pleasure than being an MP would have done. He took it home on his motor-bike and named it Warrington.

The next bit of extra-terrestrial news was also of a contest, only this time our candidate did win. Young Poppy, one of Parsley's last pups, won the Southampton Open Novice. Her owner sent us Poppy's photograph and a press account of the class. Brian said the excitement was killing him and would I kindly remove both souvenirs from the wall over Parsley's basket before they marked the wallpaper.

He was getting the bit between his teeth as regards

decorating and had started rubbing down the outside walls. In between customers that is. Not the ideal way either to run a shop or to paint a house and he looked permanently exhausted. Then we had a real stroke of luck. A couple called Pam and Bill who had been coming in for plants on and off for some weeks asked if their twelve-year-old daughter Kathryn could exercise Noah for me. Kathryn turned out to be a kind and capable rider and was soon taking Noah out regularly after school. Pam, fetching her by car one evening, looked at the mountain of washing-up in the kitchen and said, 'You could do with a hand, couldn't you? I'm free in the afternoons.'

'Oh gosh,' I said, giddy with relief and snatched meals, '*would* you? What about your own work though?' Pam already had a part-time morning job and a huge house to run.

'I've given up trying to keep the house straight,' she said. 'We gave Martin a motor-bike for his birthday and he's turned the kitchen into a pit stop. Why do boys always have to take their motor-bikes to bits?'

'I don't know. Can't you ask Martin to do it in a shed?'

Pam said it was easier to surrender to the bike than try to reason with a sixteen-year-old. She was quite right of course; I had mercifully forgotten Marcus's caveman phase. 'So I'll start tomorrow if you like,' she said. 'Come on, Kathryn let's get you home. What have you got for homework tonight?'

'Maths and geography.'

'Ooh good. I'll swap you both for the ironing?'

'It's a deal,' said Kathryn. (She went on to get good O-levels which would seem to confirm that for some children homework isn't really necessary.) 'Mum, do you know what Noah did? He's so sweet, he stopped at this gate . . .' Pam fixed me with a stiff look over the top of her glasses and said pointedly: 'This isn't going to *lead* to anything is it, Faith? Like a pony in the kitchen?'

'Well, she wouldn't take it to pieces, would she?'

'And you'd have dung, Mum,' Kathryn said. 'Good for the garden.'

'Mum doesn't want dung, love,' said Pam patiently. 'Mum

doesn't want a dismantled camshaft on the draining board either. Mum wants a quiet life.'

Although a tea lawn *is* quiet compared to Brands Hatch or the House of Commons it isn't exactly a rest cure. Pam started work the next day and within the hour we discovered we were very bad for each other. Separately we could remain composed in public, saving up the funny things people said or did to relay to our long-suffering husbands later, but together we found it impossible. It was absolutely marvellous for me to have found a soul-mate, a fellow giggler and people-watcher and one whose sense of the ridiculous was second to none. But our poor customers. One of Pam's first was a young Dutchman, a serious white-faced youth who came in for a cream tea. Pam took his order and went indoors to prepare his tray. She put the kettle on and while she was waiting for it to boil she went back to the lawn to see to another family who had just arrived. What she didn't know, and what I had forgotten to tell her, was that our electric kettle had fixed ideas about the number of hours it would work each day and if it felt at all put upon it would do a sort of emergency stop. You had to bash its socket with a knife handle to start it again. So when Pam went to make the tea she found the water still cold. 'Sorry,' I said, 'I forgot to tell you,' and I showed her the trick with the knife handle.

'I'll take that lad's tray out and he can start on his scones while it boils this time,' she said.

'Righto. I'll bring the crockery for the other family.' We carried our trays out together.

'I'm sorry to keep you waiting,' Pam said to the Dutchman. 'The kettle is taking a long time.'

'Is that so?' said the young man. He looked at the things on his tray and pointed to the cream. 'But that is not a long time, Madam, you have the cream.'

'The kettle I said, not the cream,' said Pam.

'But the cream it comes from the kettle, yes?' He gestured towards the countryside at large.

Pam saw what he was getting at a second before I did. She caught my eye and had to bite her lip. 'Excuse me,' she gulped and ran back to the kitchen. I followed and found her doubled up.

'Has that cattle boiled yet, Pam?'

'*Don't*.' She mopped her eyes. 'That poor boy – he, oh dear.'

'I know. He must think we milk a cow every time someone wants cream.'

'A *slow* cow. He looked so serious when I said the kettle's taking a long time, then when I saw the penny drop with you – oh gosh.' It was a goodish while before either of us was capable of carrying scalding hot tea to the customers.

With Pam around the teas were never a chore. She said it was like putting peanuts out for birds – hours of entertainment in exchange for food – and was soon coming in most weekday afternoons. Some days she saw to all the catering which freed me for the Garden Centre customers which in turn meant Brian could put in two or three uninterrupted hours on the house.

We had been serving teas since Easter – over four months – when one day a customer said to me, 'I see you've got your planning permission.'

'What for?' I said.

'For your teas and coffees. Look.' She fished a local paper from her shopping basket and showed me a page listing all the current planning applications and council decisions on them. Half-way down the page was our name and address and: 'Permission to serve light refreshments on Garden Centre premises. Granted.'

I borrowed the paper for a moment and took it to show Brian. 'There must be some mistake,' I said. 'We got the planning permission in April, didn't we?'

'We *thought* we did,' he said, 'but come to think of it we've never actually received anything on paper from the council, have we?'

'No, well, *forms*, but not anything that looked like a licence. Why did we think we had?'

'It was your health inspector. He said he would okay the application.'

'That's right. But of course he only *said* it – he didn't write it. This means I've been poisoning the tourists without a licence all this time.' We decided that if the council wanted to fine us retrospectively they could go ahead. If it took them four months to write 'granted' on a piece of paper it would take them years to prepare a court action during which time we would have moved.

I took the paper back to the waiting customer and we had a cosy chat about moronic civil servants. 'I'm glad they put "light" refreshments though,' I said. 'A friend of ours said my scones would sink ducks.'

'Friend?' she said. 'By the way I see your husband has made a start on the, um, on your house.'

'Go on, say it,' I said. 'The eyesore?'

'Yes, I didn't know you knew that's what people call it.'

'We call it a lot worse than that. What were you going to say about Brian painting it?'

'Only that you have to have permission from the Park authorities first. Did you know?'

'Permission to *paint your own house?*'

'Mm. You can only have permitted colours inside the Park boundary. Houses mustn't— '

'Detract from the scenery,' I finished. 'Oh well, that's reasonable. You wouldn't want a national park looking like a circus poster. Thanks for telling me anyway.'

Brian thought that permitted colouring sounded like a food additive but was pleased to hear about a rule which was for the good of the countryside. The paint we had chosen for the eyesore was the nearest we could find to army-style camouflage, a sort of slurry colour called something like Sylvan Glen. It was on the approved list so we didn't have to cart fifteen gallons back to the paint shop as we would have had to if we had chosen orange, yellow or scarlet.

Giving the bungalow a facelift was going to be the last major Garden Centre job, a cheering prospect which sustained us through the difficulties of the work itself. These were threefold. 1) We could only spare one of us for a few hours a day to do the work 2) It was a tough job, a wire brushing first then a wash down followed by a coat of fungicide, two undercoats and two topcoats 3) We were no longer young.

A day off to watch the royal wedding (next door at Gordon and Bunty's with a lovely salad lunch in the garden at half time), followed by an evening round a bonfire laid on in the village where my mother now lived, made a welcome break. Prince Charles was uncannily good at timing his arrangements; first by getting engaged so that we could find Honey, then by declaring a national holiday on the hottest day of the year when neither of us felt like serving customers, a good man.

The hot weather brought salad crops to early maturity. Tomatoes, peppers and cucumbers had to be picked twice a week and courgettes daily. To hold the crops back a bit we painted the outside of the main glasshouse with a substance called Summer Cloud. This is a brilliant invention, a shower-resistant shield which you apply in sunny weather. It admits light but cuts down the heat. At the end of the summer you can get it off easily enough with brooms tied on the end of hosepipes.

There was too much produce for our own customers so Brian asked a local greengrocer to take our surplus. It was a useful outlet. The greengrocer even collected his order so our work was reduced to just picking and weighing. He had about 200lbs of tomatoes a week and 10lbs each of the other things. He gave us 18p a pound for tomatoes, quite a good wholesale price and 20p a pound for peppers.

Sometimes I would put some of the salad stuff on the tea tables to remind people to buy more than just a cream tea. Pam used to complain there was hardly room to set out the crockery between my harvest festival displays. Most customers did buy some produce when they had finished their teas, particularly cucumbers which for some strange reason a lot of people liked warm, straight from the tropical greenhouse. 'It's the smell,' one woman explained, shoving a cucumber up her nose. 'It reminds me of summers when I was a girl.'

Pam was right about getting hours of entertainment from the customers. A surprising number, usually couples, came in to have a row. With each other that is, although if they had known that they had an audience they might have started on us. We loved quarrellers, not only for their entertainment value but because they hardly ate anything. It is extremely difficult to bicker and eat at the same time, consequently very profitable for the caterer.

We had two beauties one day. The first couple were at odds because she had been unfaithful and the second couple had locked horns over a dog called Nigger. In order to get our money's worth Pam and I resorted to low cunning. We couldn't just stand and listen nor could we be for ever replenishing their hot-water jugs so we each took a watering can and very slowly watered all the ornamental tubs round the edge of the tea lawn.

The cuckolded husband kept saying, 'With *Alexander* of all people'. He was a smarmy type, the sort of man who automatically looks at his own reflection in shop windows. Pam whispered, 'He looks like that old film star our mothers used to drool over.'

'Rudolph Valentino?'

'No, you idiot, not that far back. The one who wasn't in *Gone with the Wind*. Smug. Creepy moustache. Got it – Errol Flynn.'

'I wonder what she saw in him.'

Mrs E.F., obviously as dissatisfied with her spouse as we were, sipped her tea and looked into the distance. 'You've made me a figure of fun in the regiment,' Errol continued. 'You're not the first Alexander has taken advantage of, you know.'

'I wish you'd stop calling him Alexander,' said his wife who was young and beautiful. 'Everyone calls him Sandy. And he didn't take advantage. It was mutual.'

'Mutual? Huh. I wonder how mutual.'

'Meaning?'

'Meaning it's a feather in his cap to bed the wife of a major. I hope you'll come to your senses when we're posted.'

Frustratingly, other customers claimed our attention and we never knew whether she decided to 'come to her senses' or to leave Errol and marry Sandy.

But the other couple's tiff did have a happy ending. We picked up the tale at about the half-way stage. They had probably done the shouting, then the sulking, and were now ready to spit on their hands ready for round three. Pam laid their table, then beckoned me over for a quick rundown. 'He wants his widowed father to come and live with them,' she reported, 'but the wife doesn't.'

'Why not?'

'Don't know. Something about a dog. Watering cans?' I nodded and we filled our cans and started to drown the tubs for the second time in one afternoon.

'Nice strong cuppa, this is.' The wife offered a small olive branch.

'Aye, it is. Nice view. I like a nice view.'

'Hot.'

'Mm, hot. Nice breeze though.' They sat in silence for ages crumbling their scones and sipping tea. Get *on* with it, I thought. It worked.

'We've got to settle this once and for all, Reen. You've got to say yes or no. Dad can't stay where he is.'

'I know. I've told you my terms. He can have the spare room or he can go into sheltered housing. But if he comes to us I'm not having Nigger running loose in the garden.'

'You *like* Nigger.'

'Oh, for God's sake, Tom, grow up. We live in the middle of *Southall*. Last time Dad came to stay I nearly died of shame with him calling Nigger at the top of his voice. He's got very noisy since he went deaf. That poor Mrs Patel next door.'

'It 'ud kill Dad to get rid of Nigger.'

'You don't listen to a word I say, do you? I've never suggested getting rid of Nigger. All I ask is for Dad to call him something else.'

'But Dad's always had a Nigger. Ever since he was a boy he's called his dogs Nigger. He can't change at eighty-five.'

'Tom, we've all got to move with the times. He could call him Nigel. It's a nice name Nigel.'

'He'd forget. Even if he agreed he'd forget. Couldn't you explain to Mrs Patel?'

'No.'

Stalemate. Pam and I looked at each other and racked our brains to think of a solution. 'I'll top up their te. pot,' Pam said. 'You have a good think while I'm gone.'

I thought. All I came up with was changing the dog's name to Tigger but of course if Dad was going to forget . . . Reen had a point though. It didn't seem fair on Mrs Patel. And Tom was right too. You can't change old people. Damn it, everybody was right.

Tom and Reen drank more tea. 'You know,' said Tom, 'you've given me an idea.'

'Oh yes?'

'What you said about moving with the times. We could move house.'

'Move house? What for?'

'So as Dad could keep Nigger as Nigger. I could get a transfer to the firm's Hastings branch and Dad could take Nigger on the beach.'

'Ooh Tom.' Reen stopped messing about with her scones and began to eat properly. 'Hastings. What a lovely place to live. And of course it wouldn't matter what Dad shouted on the beach, nobody would notice what with the sea and that. A nice semi with a big garden. Here let me give you a refill, your tea's gone stone cold.'

On another occasion I unwittingly started a row between a husband and wife. A family of four, a couple with two children aged about five and six, drove in during the morning and asked for two cups of coffee and two glasses of orange juice. I put the drinks on their table together with two drinking straws for the children. When I went back to clear the table the two straws were still in their wrappers but two other straws were sticking out of the empty glasses. 'We've got our own,' said one of the children, 'better ones than yours. Longer.' And he held up a third straw identical to those in the glasses. I was about to smile politely and go away when it struck me that these were not drinking straws at all. They were cattle AI straws. Used ones. 'Crikey,' I said.

'What are you staring at?' said the mother.

'These straws. Are you staying on a farm for your holiday?'

'Yes, what of it?'

'These are cattle insemination straws. How on earth did your children get hold of them?'

'Artificial insem— you don't mean – you can't mean . . . Oh my God. In their *mouths*.' The mother went white, but I thought it might be tactless to offer her the orange juice dregs as a reviver.

'How do you know these are cattle straws?' asked the father, holding one up and looking at it with interest.

'Well, pigs have different apparatus,' I explained. 'Their semen is stored in glass jars and delivered through a rubber tube. Whereas cows are inseminated— '

'*Stop stop.*' The mother put her hands over her ears. The children began to cry and the father began to laugh. I didn't know what to do so I beat a hasty retreat to the kitchen.

When I next looked out to see if the coast was clear the parents were at it hammer and tongs, each accusing the other of sexual failings. Quite how the quarrel could have reached such proportions in so short a time was a mystery, but then people never fail to amaze. To look at them you'd never have guessed she was a cold fish nor he the type to think more of his bloody car than his wife. The children, having been deprived of their new toys, were now trawling through a litter bin, doubtless in search of more parent-provoking waste-products. I shut the door and turned the radio up until they had gone.

The school holidays brought much the same cross-section of tourists as we had had the previous season. Gnome hunters, cuttings collectors, happy families, families with teenagers, people taking study courses at summer schools, single ramblers, parties of ramblers, etc. Once we had to evict a foreign family who had the cheek to try and picnic on the tea lawn. In front of a crowd of customers they unloaded rugs, thermos flasks and food and spread themselves on the grass. I couldn't shift them because they didn't speak English and I couldn't make them understand that our garden was private property. Pam had a try in sign language. It looked as

189

though she was scolding a dog for making a mess on the carpet and they just stared at her blankly so we had to get Brian. He was plastered in paint and none too pleased to be dragged away from his work. 'Off you go,' he said, waving his paintbrush. I'm sure they didn't understand the words but he must have looked sufficiently unhinged with his torn shorts and Sylvan Glen chest to frighten them away.

But on the whole the customers were a likeable lot; we were even lucky enough to make several new friends, with people who started off as customers. There were Sheila and Bryan who told us their own social life had suffered a short setback when after a visit to the Ideal Home exhibition they bought an ecological lavatory. This horrendous contraption was supposed to convert human waste into dry, sterile fertiliser but despite having a Design Centre award it never worked. What was worse was that its failure to work was only too pungently obvious 'throughout the entire house' they recalled. In the end they had to empty it by hand, an experience which they were still trying to forget.

And there were Alan and Bunty (not to be confused with Bunty next door) who had only recently returned to England after working abroad most of their lives. When they came in to buy some plants Bunty was still mistaking a 5p coin for a dollar, and as I still looked upon any sum in double figures as a sort of brain-death we made a fine hash of things. Bunty handed me four 5p and four 10p coins to settle a bill of £4.40. I looked at the money in bewilderment. Had the government sneakily altered the currency again? 'There, um, doesn't seem to be quite enough here,' I said nervously. (Had I known then that both Bunty and Alan were ex-head teachers I would have cheerfully accepted that 60p equals £4.40.) To my surprise Bunty burst out laughing and called Alan over to supply some more money. 'You'll get us arrested,' he said. 'You should have got the hang of it by now.' He sounded exactly like Brian – not his accent, which was faintly Geordie, but his put-upon-husband air. We got chatting, then Brian joined us and in no time at all it was, 'You must come round for a drink.'

On Bank Holiday Monday we closed the shop and took a

stall at a village fête for the day. It was late when we got home and the dogs, who had been shut in the kitchen for eight hours, shot outside as soon as we opened the door. They loved summer evenings and would often go off rabbiting in the woods on their own, so when they hadn't returned by dusk we didn't worry. We had our supper, then went up the paddock to get them in. Ella and Parsley came as soon as they heard Brian whistle but there was no sign of Honey. 'It's a warm night,' Brian said, 'not like when she was lost before. She'll come home when she's hungry.'

But by bedtime Honey was still out. I phoned the main police station (village police and criminals work office hours) and apologised for troubling them. Someone took down Honey's particulars and said reassuringly, 'She'll most likely come home soon, dogs generally do. Anyway we'll phone you if anyone brings her in.' Then we went to bed, only to be woken an hour later by Honey scratching to come in.

'You old horror,' we said, 'have your dinner and go in your basket. This is positively the last time you're going out on your own.' (Little did we know. A year later Honey was missing for twenty-one days on an adventure which went down in family folklore as Honey's Last Fling.) And off we went to bed for the second time.

Next morning, as I had some shopping to do in the village, I thought I would pop in to tell the local bobby to cancel any report of a missing dog. But before I got to the police station I saw him strolling along the road. 'Hullo,' he said, 'I was just on my way to see you. They've been found.'

'*They*?' I said. 'But it was only one. Honey.'

'Two,' he said firmly. 'Good job they were wearing their headcollars.'

My heart went down like a lift. 'H . . . headcollars?' I gulped.

'I wish everybody wrote their address on their horses' headcollars,' he went on. 'It's so sensible. Saves us a lot of time.'

I didn't feel very sensible. It was quite brain-scrambling to be told that an unlost dog had suddenly become two found ponies. When had Noah and Rory escaped? How?

'You all right?' asked the constable.

'Oh, er, yes.' I swiftly pulled myself together and tried to look like someone who had been combing the neighbourhood for missing ponies. 'Thank you for finding them. Where are they?'

'In a field about a mile out.' He pointed along a road leading from the village. 'The lady who caught them opened the nearest gate and put them in.'

From an equine health point of view the helpful lady could scarcely have chosen a worse field. I found Noah and Rory ecstatically eating the grassy equivalent of hundreds of cream teas. They had to be caught quickly and tied up before they blew up. I must have lost half a stone chasing them round and round that field before I finally cornered them. It was only the fear of them getting colic that kept me going at a pace Kevin Keegan might have envied. I tied them to a tree with the baler twine all farmers leave lying around for just such emergencies and drove home, red as a beetroot and not relishing the prospect of telling Brian.

'Where *have* you been? Did you have a puncture?'

'The ponies are out,' I said and waited for World War Three to start.

'I know,' he said. 'We'll have to go and look for them.'

This was disconcerting. Having prepared my defences for 'Your blasted ponies are nothing but trouble' I wasn't ready for sympathy and co-operation. 'They've been caught,' I said. 'They're in a field about four miles away.'

'And you've come home for their bridles?'

'I've come home because if I'd left the car four miles away you'd have gone mad.'

'Me?' he said, all sweetness and light.

'Brian, are you OK? The ponies have been on the rampage, you've got to drive me out to fetch them and then you've got to find the fault in their electric fence. Why are you being so reasonable?'

'It was my fault they got out,' he said. 'I switched their fence off when we were searching for Honey last night. I must have forgotten to switch it on again.'

'But— ' I began, then changed my mind. It was nice not

being in the wrong. Even nicer was jogging home bareback, enjoying the sunshine and birdsong and clop clop of the ponies' hooves. 'Listen boys,' I said. Their ears twitched backwards. 'Don't tell Brian but I distinctly remember switching your fence back on myself. He must have pushed the switch first so when I did it I was actually switching it *off* again. What do you think of that then?' I knew my secret would be safe with them because although Brian speaks dog and cow he has never learned horse.

As soon as the school holidays ended we stopped serving teas and sold off all the lawn furniture and crockery. Although we missed some of the more colourful customers ('Don't let Grandad go to the toilet without his specs'), it was good to have some spare time. Our evenings were our own again; instead of baking there was now an orgy of reading, catching up on the backlog of books we had had to sacrifice during the summer. (I say we, for although only one of us did the baking the other one wasn't allowed a moment's peace while there was a martyr in the kitchen.)

As well as selling off the tea things we sold the tractor and the bees and one or two large mowing machines. Wherever our next move took us we didn't want the trouble and expense of transporting bulky machines again nor the hazard of moving bees. After four honeyless years we had come to the conclusion that our bees hated us and as the feeling was now mutual we watched their departure with relief. Brian was sorry to see the tractor go though – an old Fordson Major, it had been the very first item of farm equipment we had bought when we moved to the country and had seen us safely through five haymakings.

Even without the teas the Garden Centre was busy. We held a half-price sale of all summer bedding stock. People materialised out of thin air and snapped up bargain geraniums, begonias and fuchsias as fast as we could wrap them. Brian finished painting the outside of the bungalow and the transformation was so pleasing that Gordon and Bunty invited us round to drink a toast to slurry-green paint. 'Look out of the window,' they said. 'You've camouflaged it so well it hardly shows. In fact your conservatory looks lovely with all those flowering plants on the ledges.'

'We never used it for the teas, you know,' I said.

'Really?' said Bunty. 'I'd have thought people would have enjoyed having tea surrounded by plants.'

'I let them in once,' I said. 'It began to rain and I felt sorry for them. But I couldn't get them out again – they even started browsing through our books and playing with the dogs. So after that if it rained I left them out in it.'

'Very hospitable,' Gordon said drily. 'I take it your next project won't involve catering?'

Our nomadic existence was beginning to bother friends and family. The 'A' pages of their address books were a mess they complained and when were we going to Put Down Roots? Marcus, thousands of miles away in India wrote plaintively: 'Where will home be when I come back?' as if he was afraid we would move without leaving a forwarding address. (In the same letter he described a paradise where 'the bananas are virtually free and the girls astoundingly beautiful' which was nice to know and a relief that it wasn't the other way round.) Sara wanted us to move back nearer London so that she could see more of us, I wanted to stay in Devon and Brian didn't really mind where we went as long as he didn't have to live in a bungalow. Neither of us wanted a retail business again but Brian was keen to continue as a grower, particularly of glasshouse crops. We decided to take our time before deciding the next move and to explore as many alternatives as finances would allow. Meanwhile I would pick up the threads of my dog clipping again and finish my book while Brian saw to the Garden Centre and house-hunted.

Sylvia, my cream-tea mentor and animal-sanctuary friend, asked me if I would like to attend some of the autumn pony sales with her, now that I had some spare time. With some trepidation, for I hate all animal markets, I said I would go to one and see what it was like before committing myself. Pony sales are held each autumn in six different towns on the edge of the moor. On the day I went to my first one it was raining which didn't lighten the prevailing gloom. Sylvia and several sanctuary helpers were there and four committee members of the Dartmoor Livestock Protection Society. Also present were two RSPCA inspectors and a ministry vet.

Approximately three hundred crossbred ponies (there are no pure bred Dartmoor ponies running on Dartmoor) were herded into pens. Some were unweaned foals separated from their mothers and heart-rending to listen to. Others ranged from yearlings to aged mares whose stomachs were distorted by malnutrition and worms. All were frightened and hungry. There was no food or water in any of the pens.

I stood by the auction ring with a friend of Sylvia's, a vicar's wife called Mary, and through a blur of tears watched a small foal bundled roughly into the ring by a drover wielding a stick. The foal was cream-coloured with a black mane and tail and was no bigger than a labrador. Shivering with fright, he raised his tiny face to the sky and called piteously for his mother. A butcher opened the bidding at three pounds. There were no opposing bids so the auctioneer said 'sold for three pounds' and out went the foal to await transportation to an abattoir. More foals came and went the same way, every one of them destined for slaughter. The moorland farmers who had bred them stood around in groups, talking and joking among themselves, completely unmoved. A meat buyer from a safari park pointed to a thin foal he had bought and called out 'Elevenses for a lion?' and they all fell about laughing.

'Why do you come?' I asked Mary. She was too upset to reply but stumbled away and beckoned me to follow her. We found Sylvia talking to the butcher who had bought the cream-coloured foal. Money changed hands and Sylvia slipped into a 'killer' pen (where the meat animals wait) and gently removed the foal to an empty pen.

'What's happening?' I said.

Mary said, 'I think Sylvia has bought one. Let's hope so.'

Meanwhile, the DLPS members were walking up and down between the pens inspecting each animal as thoroughly as possible in the mêlée and occasionally conferring with the ministry vet. As the day wore on I began to see why the two charities' presence was so necessary and how each complemented the other. The sanctuary would (if funds allowed) buy ponies which were too young or too weak to endure more stress. The DLPS, on the other hand, whose general policy is not to rescue and maintain animals but to eradicate the causes of exploitation, would try to ensure that no sick animal was allowed to suffer the hardship of a long truck journey after the sale. The society would either purchase the pony and have it put down immediately or would draw the vet's attention to its condition and see that he ordered the owner to withdraw it from the sale. This procedure has obvious drawbacks. Any owner unfeeling enough to send a sick animal to market would be unlikely to give it proper care and attention once it was back on his premises.

At the end of the harrowing day I no longer needed to ask 'why do you come' but I did wonder if I would ever develop the strength of character and the courage to stand up to the dealers, drovers and breeders. For of course they detested animal welfare organisations. It spoilt their fun having 'they old do-gooders' around.

I travelled back with Sylvia, pleased that she had bought a foal and grieving for the ones we had watched being loaded into slaughterhouse lorries. She called the little scrap Merlin and started him on mare's milk substitute as soon as he was safely home. No safari park lion would have Merlin for elevenses after all.

Other sales followed, the worst being Bampton where the pony auction is actually considered a tourist attraction and is part of the traditional Bampton Fair. Hopefully it will only be a matter of time before this degrading spectacle will, like bear-baiting, be seen only in history books.

It was a relief when the sales ended, not least for Brian who had had to mind the shop on my days out. Now he could go out with maps and agents' particulars to look for a place for us. He viewed all sorts of businesses and would come home full of enthusiasm until common sense told him that just because someone else was running a successful boatyard or sawmill or trout farm, it didn't mean he could. At that time there didn't seem to be any horticultural businesses for sale in our price range so we had to look for alternatives.

In the meantime I finished revising my manuscript and sent it away to be typed. 'It had better be worth it,' Brian said, reeling when he saw the estimate. 'We've bought cars for less than that.'

'Of course it'll be worth it,' I said. 'It'll make a fortune this will. You wait.' (He is still waiting.) And by way of supplicating the gods I offered to give him a hand shifting some boulders which a passing lorry had dislodged from our boundary wall. Unfortunately the gods were in a foul mood and demanded a blood sacrifice – well, not quite blood but a sprained right wrist. Brian bound it up for me with a comfrey poultice and a few kind words. 'It could have been worse,' he said. 'At least it waited until you'd finished your writing.'

The swelling went down quickly and I was able to carry on more or less normally with my other hand. Next day I went out riding on Noah, a foolish thing to do because it was Remembrance Day and there was a brass band parading through the village. Noah had never heard a brass band and seemed nervous so I dismounted and stood by his side watching it go by. Noah was very good until some oompah-pah instrument came too close for comfort. Up he went on his back legs, then down again – on my toes. He is no lightweight.

Brian did his nut when I limped in. 'Oh shut up,' I said when he had run out of adjectives. 'Shut up and make me another poultice.'

'You need a ball and chain. A straitjacket. *Two* accidents in twenty-four hours – are you trying to get into the *Guinness Book of Records*? For God's sake, stay indoors before you lose any more limbs.'

I took things easy for a day or two but my foot still hurt quite a lot. Brian thought I had better have it X-rayed in case something was broken so I phoned a doctors' group practice in Exeter and asked the receptionist if there were any appointments free in the foreseeable future. 'Oh yes,' she said, 'but I'm afraid you'll have to make do with Dr So and So. All the other doctors are booked for days ahead.'

I must have been mad not to heed the implication of this. Blithely I limped into the waiting room and sat down. A grandmotherly woman with her arm in a sling next to me said, 'My, you are in the wars, aren't you? Have you hurt your wrist?'

'No,' I said. 'Well, yes I have, but I've come about my foot. What have you come for?' Soon we were swapping notes. She had sprained her wrist so I showed her how to apply a comfrey poultice, unwinding my own green-streaked bandage to demonstrate. Then she was called in. Another woman with a little girl took her place, the child carrying something in a cardboard box. 'It's her budgie,' said the woman to the curious waiting patients. 'We've got to go to the vet's after here.'

'What's the matter with your birdie, little girl?' asked an old man.

'He's going to have his nails cut,' said the child. 'Do you want to see him?'

'No, Julie,' said the mother, 'you can't open the box in here. He'll fly away.'

'Oh, all right,' said Julie obediently. There was a collective sigh of relief. 'But you can listen to him if you like,' she offered. The old man put his ear to the box. 'He sounds lively enough,' he said. 'Have you had him long?'

'Ever since he was an egg,' said Julie proudly. The room rocked with laughter. Then I was called in. The doctor, who had a cross face, said, 'Shut the door, please,' as if he didn't like hearing people laughing. I shut the door and sat down.

Before I could start telling him about my foot he caught sight of my bandaged wrist. 'So it was *you*,' he said grimly. It was so much like a line from a corny melodrama it made me giggle. 'Take that disgusting bandage off and drop it in the bin.'

'Hold on a minute' – Old Bossy Boots wasn't having my crêpe bandage which had cost 89p – 'I've hurt my foot.'

'Then, may I ask,' he said coldly, 'why you are presenting a vile-looking dressing on your *wrist*? Referred pain perhaps?'

'No. I did hurt my wrist but that's not what I've come about. I want you to have a look at my foot. It scrunches when I put my weight on it.' I slipped off my shoe.

He ignored the proffered foot. 'It was you, wasn't it, telling

Mrs Elton the best treatment for a sprained wrist is a comfrey poultice?'

'Comfrey is a very effective— '

'Comfrey went out with leeches.'

My eyes started to water with the effort of not laughing. I could see Mr Leech in a dinner jacket arm in arm with the dainty Miss Comfrey clad in a low-cut green dress . . .

'. . . and I'll thank you *not* to hold surgeries in my waiting room. Making the patients laugh.'

Oh dear. So it was a crime to make patients laugh. 'It wasn't me,' I said. 'It was a budgie in a cardboard box.'

He gave me a long cold stare but didn't ask what budgie or for any explanation. I could see why the receptionist had said, 'You'll have to make do with Dr So and So.' Eventually he sighed and said, 'What's wrong with your foot?'

But even as I began to tell him how Noah had reared and landed on my toes I could sense he wasn't really interested. I rather suspected he must have been away when they did feet at medical school because all he could suggest by way of treatment was a metatarsal support. 'You can buy them at the chemist's,' he said.

'I'd like to have an X-ray. Something might be broken.'

He dismissed this with a wave of his Parker pen with a real gold nib – the only thing about him that I liked. 'Feet,' he said pompously, 'have a remarkable capacity for self-repair.'

I felt sorry for any geriatrics he might have on his list. Feet, as our lovely old coach party ladies demonstrated, are about the only parts of bodies which *don't* repair themselves. 'So that's it then?' I asked, feeling a real lemon with my foot waving in the air. He hadn't risked actually touching it even though it had been washed and powdered for the occasion. 'Just a metatarsal support?'

'Yes. The instructions will be on the wrapper. Of course *you* may prefer to hang it round your neck but it's usually worn on the foot. Good day.'

Up yours, mate, I thought as I stormed out. Minutes later I thought of all sorts of sarcastic things I could have said but it was too late. 'He was horrible,' I said to Brian who was waiting in the car, 'absolutely horrible.'

'I expect you rubbed him up the wrong way,' Brian said mildly. 'Allopaths don't like being lectured on homoeopathy.'

'I didn't mention homoeopathy. Honestly, Brian, he was awful – didn't even examine my foot. Pull up at the chemist's would you – I've got to try a support thing. Anyway when we move we must find a different doctor, I don't want to go back there again.'

'It's a group practice. If you don't like that one you can always see one of the others.'

'No, his partners must be pretty dim or they would have slung him out long ago.' (Four years later, still scrunching, I was fortunate enough to find a proper healer who re-aligned the bones and made my foot as good as new.)

'OK we'll change. But let's find ourselves a house first.'

One Sunday morning in the dead of winter Brian was looking through the papers when he spotted a photograph in a house agent's advert. It looked like a crusty loaf in a thick fog. 'I think I know where this is,' he said and opened an ordnance survey map of Dartmoor.

'Even if you do know where it is do you really want to live in a loaf? It looks very dark.'

'The picture's terrible,' he agreed, 'but then newspaper photos often are. Shall we go and see if we can find it?'

'No thanks. There's no address and no price. Let's wait until the agents are open tomorrow.'

'I'm going. Come on dogs – walkies.'

'I'll send a search party when it gets dark. Cheerio.' And throwing some more wood on the fire I went back to the papers.

An hour later Brian reappeared. 'Come with me,' he said. 'I've found us a house. With stairs.'

After a drive across open moorland we freewheeled through two stone pillars and down a muddy cart track and there, crouched in the fold of some hills, was a thatched cottage. Not a chocolate-box cottage but a sturdy unpretentious Devon longhouse – the long in this instance seeming more of a courtesy title as it was the shortest longhouse imaginable. Built of granite in the early 1500s it had undergone just one major change since then. To replace the original ventilation slits, small windows had been put it – charming windows with little granite eyebrows to channel off the rainwater. The cottage had been empty for some time and one of the upstairs windows had been boarded in giving the front the impression of a face with a huge welcoming wink.

We 'gained entry' as they say in crime reports – it's a shamefully easy step from house-hunting to house-breaking – and inhaled the musty interior with all the appreciation of people who had spent two years in a modern bungalow. It was like a homecoming. Brian sighed happily and got out his penknife. 'Do you realise this was here *before* the *Mary Rose* was built?' he said scraping away at a plastered-in beam. Predictably, the inglenook and bread oven had been 'modernised' and all the paintwork which should have been white was a punishing shade of blue. Leaving him to excavate, I went up the winding stairs to see what sort of a view we would be buying this time. Deep recessed windows looked out to a scene so pastoral the original inhabitants could have come back and not known four hundred years had passed. The only other house to be seen (*circa* 1000 and mentioned in the Domesday Book we later learned) lay in a dip below to the right while to the left there was a deciduous wood, a small river, and some very satisfactory sheep meadows disappearing into the distance.

I clattered down the wooden stairs to report that the view came up to scratch, but Brian had vanished. A muffled reply to my, 'Hoi, where are you?' came from a cow byre leading off the main room. (Longhouses are separated into animal and human quarters, divided by a short passageway.) The byre made us gasp. Nothing except the now corrugated-iron roof had been touched for centuries. There were massive granite walls, oak partitions and a stone floor sloping to a central dung channel. (An expert who later came to list the place as being of outstanding historic interest said it was the finest dung channel he had ever seen.) We had quite a job to find the floor on this first visit. The last occupant of the cottage had been a hoarder; everything from discarded shoes to false teeth had been chucked into the byre until the mountain of rubbish reached literally to the roof struts. One of the treasures we unearthed was a box full of women's magazines dating back to 1912. It was hard to tear ourselves away from this diversion and continue the tour of inspection.

The place needed a lot of attention, it had been so neglected that weeds had encroached right up to the walls of the house, there was no kitchen as such and it needed replumbing and rewiring. Some of the upstairs wooden floors would have to be replaced and central heating installed to drive out the damp.

But even in this state, the enduring appeal of the granite cottage left us in no doubt that this was the place for us. And fanciful or not, it seemed as though the cottage was welcoming its new occupants, approving the changes we planned for it. There would be masses of flowers encircling the house with honeysuckle and clematis sprinting up the walls, insects would hum tidily in and out of the runner beans while butterflies – not too many because of the cabbages – flitted here and there. All the little windows would be wide open to let the sunshine in, the sills displaying pots of gaily-coloured geraniums – *unlabelled* geraniums for extra enjoyment.

Brian said he wondered what sorts of things would do best at an altitude several hundred feet higher than any place we had lived in before and I said llamas because I had recently read an article about a man who had started a llama herd on Dartmoor. Apparently their wool is in great demand for home spinning and weaving. Brian didn't dismiss the idea of llamas which surprised me until I realised he hadn't been listening. He was mentally grubbing out a box hedge and green-manuring the beds. 'Delphiniums against that wall,' he murmured. 'Pinks and pansies here and here . . .'

Well, two can play at that game. I went back to my llamas. The article had said that they thrived on Dartmoor.